VGM Opportunities Series

OPPORTUNITIES IN
COUNSELING AND DEVELOPMENT CAREERS

Neale J. Baxter

Revised by
Mark Uri Toch
Philip A. Perry

VGM Career Horizons
a division of *NTC Publishing Group*
Lincolnwood, Illinois USA

Cover Photo Credits:

Upper left courtesy of Loyola University Chicago Medical Center.
Upper right copyright © Dennis MacDonald/Photo Network.
Lower left and lower right photos by Robert Catania. Courtesy of Loyola University
Chicago.

Library of Congress Cataloging-in-Publication Data

Baxter, Neale.
    Opportunities in counseling and development careers / Neale J.
Baxter. — Revised / by Mark Uri Toch and Philip A. Perry.
      p.   cm. — (VGM opportunities series)
    Includes bibliographical references.
    ISBN 0-8442-4688-3 (alk. paper). — ISBN 0-8442-4689-1 (pbk. :
alk. paper)
    1. Counseling—Vocational guidance.   I. Toch, Mark Uri.
II. Perry, Philip A.   III. Title.   IV. Series.
BF637.C6B285   1997
361'.06'02373—dc21   96-52397
                                              CIP

Published by VGM Career Horizons, a division of NTC Publishing Group
4255 West Touhy Avenue
Lincolnwood (Chicago), Illinois 60646-1975, U.S.A.
© 1997 by NTC Publishing Group. All rights reserved.
No part of this book may be reproduced, stored in a retrieval
system, or transmitted in any form or by any means,
electronic, mechanical, photocopying, recording or otherwise,
without the prior permission of NTC Publishing Group.
Manufactured in the United States of America.

7 8 9 0 VP 9 8 7 6 5 4 3 2 1

CONTENTS

ABOUT THE AUTHOR

Neale Baxter has published widely on a great variety of occupations, including two previous VGM books, *Opportunities in Federal Government Careers* and *Opportunities in State and Local Government Careers.* His award-winning articles have appeared in such diverse publications as *The Occupational Outlook Quarterly, The Monthly Labor Review, Career World,* and the *Washington Post.* He is currently the managing editor of a magazine published by the federal government. He earned a bachelor's degree from Manhattan College, a master's from Purdue University, and a Ph.D. from the University of North Carolina at Chapel Hill. He lives in Virginia with his wife, Anne, and his children, Kathleen and Tom.

Philip A. Perry wrote this revision. Perry is a journalist who has written on health care, business, and management subjects since 1989. He was senior editor of *Health Care Strategic Management,* a national health care newsletter, for two years, reporting and writing on hospital management trends, health reform, management information systems, generic pharmaceuticals, and other topics. Among his current assignments is writing medical purchasing news for American Hospital Publishing, Inc., Chicago. He is also the author of *Opportunities in Mental Health Careers.* His B.A. is from Northwestern University and his M.S.J. is from Medill School of Journalism.

ACKNOWLEDGMENTS

Thanks are due, as always, to Kathleen, Tom, and Anne, who provide a reason to work on books like this and welcome respites from working on them.

Many people generously shared their experience and knowledge with me, thus making this book possible. The twenty-two experts quoted in Chapter 19 must be mentioned first: Olie Ahlquist, Les Blankenship, William A. Bryan, Jon Dalton, Tom Gertz, Ken Hoyt, Dorothy Jenkins, John Keyser, Richard LaFon, Dennis Martin, Carl McDaniels, Frederick E. Menz, Fred Otte, Duane Parker, Bill Richardson, Dorothy Thomas, Jean A. Thompson, Edwin A. Whitfield, Richard R. Wilmarth, Gaynelle Wilson, Jim Wilson, and George Wright. In addition to the statements attributed to them there, they provided me with hundreds of leads and innumerable pieces of information that have been quietly incorporated into the text.

Among the many other counselors, researchers, and association professionals who were also helpful are the following: Bill Abbot, Jim Banning, Carol Bonnie, Douglas Brown, Frank Burtnett, Mike Chrin, Dan Crowe, Sandra Dennis, Jack Donohue, Bertie Firestone, Wilton Fowler, Janet Fumanti, Jan Gelardo, Daniel Hecker, Barbara Huffman, Thuman Huynh, Gayla Keese, Joanne Kipnis, Steve Krammer, Dannielle LeMolle, Tom Leif, Frank Lisnoou, Paul Lubben, Susan Mason, Joe Maxwell, Madelin McClean, Elizabeth McGregor, Kay Monks, Ludmilla Murphy, Rhea Nagle, Carol Neiman, Helen Paton, Bill Pierce, Georgine Pion, JoAnn Puerling, Bonnie Raines, Jim Reed, T. F. Rigger,

Lynn Slavenski, Mary Stanley, Charles L. Thompson, Steven Townsend, Nancy Whelan, Viki Wildermuth, Michael Witkin, Ray Woodruff, and Sylvia Nissenoff, the librarian at American Counseling Association, who pointed me in new directions more than once when I encountered a dead end.

Some books that were helpful to me are listed in Appendix B. Mention should be made here, however, of authors and speakers whose works were especially informative: F. Stephen Alexander, Richard Bolles, Richard W. Daniel, Thomas K. Fagan, Norman C. Gysbers, Joseph W. Hollis, J. Anthony Humphreys, Earl J. More, Donald Mortensen, Robert D. North, Elizabeth Ogg, John J. Pietrofesa, Daniel Robinson, Alan Schmuller, Bruce Shertzer, Michael Stanton, Joy Stapp, Shelley C. Stone, E.L. Tolbert, Arthur E. Traxler, Richard A. Wantz, William J. Weikel, and C. Gilbert Wrenn.

Special thanks are due to the counselors who took time from their busy schedules to discuss their work in detail: Mary Ashton, Fred Hechlinger, Ellissia Price, Linda Seligman, and Francis A. Thomas. For the 1997 edition, special thanks to the American Counseling Association's (ACA) Jennifer Sachs and librarian Sylvia Nissenoff. Also Dr. Earl Ginter of ACA's medical committee, who provided information and arranged for interviews. Many individuals in different specialties also helped to update facts and figures. Interviews with Dr. Joseph Scalise, Linda Lawless, and others were valuable additions. Dr. Michael Leahy of Michigan State University and Dr. Edna Szymanski of the University of Wisconsin assisted with information on rehabilitation. Dr. Deborah Davis provided information about college counseling. Many others too numerous to mention are also deserving of thanks.

The chapters on the nature of the work for different kinds of counselors are based on their comments, although some adjustments were made both to protect the privacy of their clients and to fit the format of this work. Despite their assistance, some errors may have crept into these or other chapters; in such cases the fault is entirely my own.

FOREWORD

- Helping people grow in spite of changing circumstances, personal crises, or their resources.
- Helping people through the transition from one stage in life to the next.
- Helping people understand themselves, their abilities and potential.
- Helping people set goals, overcome barriers, access resources and plan fulfilling, productive lives.

That's what professional counselors do and it is what you can do if you become a professional counselor. As a professional counselor, you will have the opportunity to help people of all ages and from all walks of life, to guide them through personal, social, educational, and career challenges on the journey to reach their goals and aspirations.

Counseling itself is as old as the history of the human race. Some of the greatest scholars and thinkers throughout time have shared their wisdom by counseling others. It is only in this century, however, that professional counseling has become a formal profession recognized in its own right. Today, professional counselors can be found working at all levels in schools and universities, hospitals, mental health agencies, rehabilitation facilities, business and industry, correctional institutions, religious organizations, community centers, and private practice.

As people's lives have changed throughout the years, so has their need for personal growth and fulfillment. That is why the field of professional counseling is such an exciting one and why we expect the profession to grow significantly in the next millenium.

What distinguishes professional counselors from psychiatrists, psychologists, and social workers is that counselors often focus on wellness and prevention, helping people make decisions, solve problems, and adjust to change before they are in crisis or facing serious problems. Professional counselors also are trained to diagnose and treat all types of mental illness and work with mentally ill clients to help them achieve optimum mental health. In addition, professional counselors work with other mental health professionals, teachers, doctors, clergy, community leaders, and many others to care for people and ensure the total wellness of mind, body, and spirit.

As you consider pursuing work in the field of professional counseling, I urge you to talk to other counselors about their work and to use this book to gain a greater understanding of how you can join a growing profession. The possibilities for you are endless and the opportunities boundless. To be a counselor, you will need to put your heart and soul into caring for others. You will give much, but you will get even more.

Gail P. Robinson, Ph.D., NCC
President, 1996–1997
American Counseling Association

CHAPTER 1

COUNSELING, A CARING PROFESSION

If you choose a counseling career, you'll join a profession that is now the life's work of more than two hundred thousand Americans. As a society we've given more attention to the total well-being of our people. Some want counseling to help them through hard times; others seek help to make the best possible decisions about school, jobs, family, and personal crises. For thousands of years, the counselor's role was filled by clergy, elders, or kinfolk, but within the past fifty years, a new profession has developed and claimed a significant expertise. In that time, psychology matured as a science and we've witnessed the specialization of all professions. Counselors found new niches in education, mental health, rehabilitation, and family therapy, to name a few. While some of the new counseling specialties are developmental—helping people reach their full potential in today's vibrant society—others are concerned with the harmful side effects of modern life: stress, violence, and broken relationships.

Counselors work quietly to help people find a direction in their lives, perhaps through education or a career choice. They help restore a sense of order and purpose to troubled people's lives. Counselors care about people. They seek methods or processes to help people help themselves. Within a trusting relationship, they search for ways to show clients how to deal with challenges.

Nearly all states now recognize counseling as a profession and provide for professional certification—similar to lawyers' bar exams or physicians' credentialing requirements. At the time this was written, 41 states had passed licensing laws for counseling. Universities train counselors with advanced degree programs in their specialties.

Many counselors work in schools, and seven of ten counselors were school counselors in 1996. Others work in private practices by themselves or with a few colleagues. But while work settings vary, the basic skills are similar. Counselors combine careful listening skills with the ability to give practical and appropriate responses to problem situations. At their best, counselors act as a trusted friend, carefully listening and tendering reasoned advice.

Counselors of the nineties and the 21st century face some new challenges, as a special issue of the *Journal of Counseling and Development,* November/December, 1995, chronicled in a round-up of commentary from experts gathered by editors Jane Myers and Dr. Edwin Herr in all counseling specialties. Among their findings:

- Career counselors are challenged by the global shifts of economies, by the change from a world of factory work to a world of offices and "knowledge work." They'll have to help their clients find a career path in this new world of work.
- School counselors will need to help pupils from the new kinds of families that make up America, not just traditional working families, but single-parent families, low-income families, immigrant families, and minorities.
- College counselors will need to be able to help students in new ways: career choice; the adjustment to life in a diverse, new campus community, possibly more diverse than home; and health issues like AIDS, substance abuse, etc.
- Family counselors working in the United States find themselves in a society with a 50 percent divorce rate, stepfamilies

involving one-third of all children born in the past decade, and high levels of domestic abuse and violence.

- Rehabilitation counselors, whose profession emerged to serve workers' compensation needs and the 600,000 injured veterans of World War II, now are turning to additional tasks with clients who have varying kinds of challenges, not just physical disabilities but developmental, and also addictive personalities.
- Mental health counselors are studying better ways to diagnose patients and are trying to offer preventive care; they seek mental health services that are recognized as necessary on a par with medical services, and paid for by appropriate private and public insurers.
- New counseling specialties will grow to meet current needs: addictions counselors to help the estimated 4 to 20 percent of Americans who are addicted to alcohol or drugs; gerontological counselors will be needed to help the growing ranks of the aged (by 2050, half of the population will be over 50, with may more senior citizens than at present) with their special needs.

In a pioneering book on counseling first published in the thirties, Rollo May asked the question, What makes a good counselor?

> "The superficial qualities of the good counselor are self-evident," he wrote. "... the ability to be at ease in other people's company, a capacity to empathize, and other characteristics ... These qualities ... can be acquired to a great extent.... But to penetrate more deeply into the problem, what differentiates a good counselor from a poor one?... Freud stated that the quality which is essential is 'inherent insight into the human soul—first of all into the unconscious layers of his own soul—and practical training.' This 'practical training' means the ability to escape from the tendency to counsel on the basis of one's own more or less rigid prejudices."

This practical training for men and women who choose counseling for a career has advanced to the point where there are many good graduate-level programs to choose from. These programs combine classroom learning with internships and practical experience under supervision. The insight that comes with experience and through self-analysis or therapy in the course of education and the early work years are considered vital to how counselors develop their abilities.

What is the right level of service to the public through counseling? That is a difficult question that is being answered through market forces and legislation by state and federal governments. At the present, the best estimates are that counseling will continue to be a growing profession through the next ten years. In some specialties, growth will be greater than average. However, many counselors who enter the profession later move on to teaching or other careers, and their field will continue to change and evolve, so new counselors are always needed.

With so many subspecialties developing, counseling as an occupation is not easily defined. You can, however, look at what individual counselors do. Chapters is this book describe several individual counselors in a variety of job settings. Basic facts are gathered here about the broad specialties, such as school, rehabilitation, mental health, and career counseling.

You can take the next step yourself, whether it's going to see counselors and discuss with them your career plans, writing to colleges to find out about their course offerings and degrees, or taking other steps to explore how you match your interests with the many possibilities that exist in counseling and development.

CHAPTER 2

VARIETIES OF COUNSELING

In the multitude of counselors there is safety.

—The Bible

Counseling is not a static profession. It must keep up with the times, developing strategies and methods to help people cope with new challenges while remaining true to the techniques that have allowed counselors to treat traditional problems and challenges as well. As in other professions, signs of change are everywhere: the guidance office down the school corridor has become a counseling center. Weekly news magazines carry advertisements that promote counseling programs for anorexia nervosa, alcoholism, and a host of other conditions.

An increased sense of professional recognition seems to be coming about. The legislatures in almost every state, for example, have passed laws licensing counselors. More and more counselors are joining professional organizations. The American Counseling Association (ACA) now boasts over 60,000 members. With this large a constituency, the ACA and other counseling organizations have impact on regulations and laws governing the counseling profession.

The changing professional climate means that a person who becomes a counselor will have a great many more career opportunities than were once possible.

Guidance—as shown in the chapter on counseling's past—originated in programs that helped people choose careers and soon became tied to schools. It has grown to include counseling on a wide array of concerns and has moved into a variety of settings, including social agencies, major corporations, and private practices.

Looking back, the transformation of guidance into counseling seems almost inevitable. Just as pioneers clearing new land cut down trees only to discover rocks and boulders, counselors working on the educational and career development of students soon learned that young people had other concerns that a counselor could help with, concerns with family, drug abuse, or normal development. Counselors began to work on these problems in addition to their other duties. Naturally, counselors who developed skills in aiding students with such problems could also help others. And so counselors increasingly found positions beyond the schoolhouse door, often specializing in fields such as employment, rehabilitation, or mental health.

TYPES OF COUNSELORS

There were about 165,000 counselors employed in the mid-1990s. Elementary and secondary school counselors made up the largest percentage of these counselors, and this trend should continue. Other types of counselors include the following:

Career counselor
Certified mental health counselor
Child development specialist
College admissions counselor
College counselor
Community agency counselor
Community mental health counselor
Counseling psychologist
Family therapist

Gerontological counselor
Human development counselor
Intervention specialist
Job counselor
Marriage and family therapy counselors
Mental health counselor
Prison counselor
Professional counselor
Public offender counselor
Rehabilitation counselor
Substance abuse counselor
Vocational counselor
Vocational rehabilitation counselor

The number of counselors working outside educational institutions has grown to the point that the nature of their work cannot be described simply in terms of school, even when the change in emphasis in school counseling—from testing and educational programs to the resolution of behavioral concerns—is taken into account. North Carolina's Department of Public Instruction summarizes the universals of counseling when it says a guidance program had three components: learning to live, learning to learn, and learning to make a living.

FUNCTIONS OF COUNSELORS

No matter where they work, counselors use individual and group counseling techniques to help people with a wide range of personal, social, career, and educational needs according to the American Counseling Association. As Frank Burtnett said when he was assistant executive director of the Association, "Counselors help people work with a concern before it becomes a problem or crisis." For example, counselors help people with stress; examine marital and family conflicts and family communication; adjust and cope with problems created by accident, illness, or other disabling misfortune; and obtain career counseling that takes into account the person's education, training, work history, interest, skills, and aptitudes. Often counselors must administer tests and interpret their results in order to help individuals learn about their strengths, weaknesses, and potential. Generally counselors concentrate on prevention or development, but some counselors specialize in remedial services. And one of the counselor's most important functions is to refer people to other sources of assistance when their problems are outside the scope of his or her specialized skills.

Another way of describing the functions of a counselor is to say that he or she intervenes to benefit the individual. W. H. Morril, E. R. Oetling, and J. C. Hurst developed a model to show the nature of the interventions counselors make. They note that the target of the intervention can be the individual, the primary group (the people the individual is close to), an associational group (people who share a concern), and the institution or community. The purpose of the intervention may be remediation, prevention, or development. And the method of intervention may be direct service; consultation with and training of people who will work with the individual; or various media, such as announcements, pamphlets, newspaper articles, and online databases.

COUNSELING SERVICES AND SETTINGS

The range of services provided by counselors is wide, although individual counselors are specialized. Rehabilitation counselors, for example, help the disabled become self-sufficient. To do this, however, they must first evaluate the client's condition and potential in far more detail than a school counselor usually does. Similarly, employment counselors might suggest specific jobs to a client and contact potential employers rather than provide only the general career information that a student needs. And mental health counselors must work closely with psychiatrists, psychologists, clinical social workers, and psychiatric nurses on a far more regular basis than does the school-based counselor.

Among the problems that counselors are more likely to deal with outside the schools than in them are physical and vocational rehabilitation, unemployment and underemployment, reentering school or work, parenting, child abuse, marital and family relationships, career changes, retirement, aging, bereavement, institutionalization, and spiritual concerns.

The nature of a counselor's work is conditioned by the work setting; typically, counselors outside the schools do more casework with individuals or small groups than do school counselors. The setting can also present unique problems. For example, everyone in a school will generally have the best interests of the student at heart; a counselor employed by a large corporation, on the other hand, must take both the worker being counseled and the good of the company into account.

Despite the growing numbers of counseling specialties, it should be stressed that the divisions are not watertight. For example, when counselors in community colleges were asked what would benefit them most, the second-most-common response was training in providing career counseling to the mature adult, which is, of course, one of the major concerns of employment counselors. And having the time to perform behavioral counseling would help school counselors prevent problems before they arise.

A counselor's work has many cycles. The day, the week, the year, the individual case history—each has peaks and valleys that shape the occupation. The following chapters each look at a counseling occupation within a different framework: the annual cycle of a high school counselor, a day in the life of an elementary school counselor, a single case history for a rehabilitation counselor in private practice, and an interview with a mental health counselor in private practice. No one of them tells all there is to learn about the nature of counseling. Together, however, they give a fair representation of the major activities of professional counselors.

CHAPTER 3

HIGH SCHOOL COUNSELORS: SQUEEZING A YEAR INTO TEN MONTHS

But where's the man who counsel can bestow,
Still pleas'd to teach, and yet not proud to know.

—Alexander Pope

Oakton High School is surrounded by new housing developments in one of the fastest-growing areas of the country. It is a major part of the lives of more than twenty-five hundred students —the scene of their triumphs and defeats in athletics and social events as well as academics. Throughout her career—about twenty-five years—Mary Ashton (recently retired) has been a part of it, first as a teacher, then as a counselor, and finally as director of guidance services. As director, she has more administrative duties than many counselors. Early in the school year, for example, she must review the objectives developed by each regular counselor. Students are assigned to Oakton's counselors alphabetically, so that each counselor works with students from all four grades. Ms. Ashton has found that this arrangement keeps the counselors up-to-date on the many different kinds of information that the students request. Another advantage of this system is that all the children in a family have the same counselor. Ms. Ashton also assigns special duties to counselors, such as acting as liaison to disabled students or a particular grade level.

In addition to administering the guidance program, Mary Ashton counsels individuals and families, although a review of her annual calendar does not show much of this side of her work. For example, she counsels students who enter the school under special circumstances, such as a return from a mental institution. She also takes over the counseling sessions of staff members who are called into crisis situations. Every referral of a student to therapy or special education classes requires consultation with her. And because she is well known in the neighborhood as a result of her long association with the school, parents sometimes call her directly with concerns that may require counseling.

Although Mary Ashton's duties thus differ somewhat from those of a typical counselor, they still reflect the rhythm of the high school year. Besides, as many would be quick to proclaim, no counselor is typical anyway.

No matter what calendars say, school years begin in the fall, which means August for Mary Ashton. She has the counseling center largely to herself for a couple of weeks before the regular counselors return. During the brief spell between the end of summer school and the beginning of the fall semester, she is concerned with the registration of students who have moved into the district since June, the schedules of students who attended summer school, and the freshman orientation program. She also attends to the needs of rising seniors who plan to apply either to one of the service academies or for ROTC scholarships. These students see her filled with hopeful anxiety. Less hopeful are others who often come into the counseling center at this time of year: former students who dropped out of school before graduating. Most often, returning to high school would be a bad idea for these older students, so Ms. Ashton talks over other possibilities with them, such as taking the GED exam or attending a nearby community college. In many cases she finds that these people have not worked in a field that made full use of their aptitudes, and she is able to direct them toward apprenticeship or other training programs that they would probably find more satisfying than high school academics.

In September, school is in full swing. The counseling staff screens newcomers to identify those who would benefit from special education classes. Counselors also distribute information booklets concerning colleges to the seniors during September and conduct sessions for the juniors on the same subject. Whenever information is given to a group of students, as in these cases, individuals often request conferences to further explore the issue. Parents, too, often confer with Ms. Ashton to discuss their student's placement or future plans.

College plans also bulk large in October, the month when Oakton holds a college fair with exhibits and presentations for more than three hundred schools. So many institutions send representatives that students need help deciding which ones to learn about. October is also PSAT month, generating a good deal of what Ms. Ashton calls *administrivia* having to do with room assignments, the recruitment of proctors, and the review of application forms. The PSAT, or Preliminary Scholastic Aptitude Test, is a practice test given to those who plan to take the SAT (Scholastic Aptitude Test) for college admission. While the PSAT is taken mostly by juniors, the freshmen and some seniors also take tests at this time. The freshmen take a differential aptitude test. Some seniors take a minimum competency examination that all Virginia high school students must pass in order to graduate. Students usually pass the exam during their sophomore year, but it must be administered again for those who failed and for students who moved into the state after the exam was last given. Planning for the sophomores' career exploration activities also occurs this month.

All the counseling and administrative tasks related to college admissions continue to require attention during November. While the seniors worry about where they will be next year, many of their youngest classmates—the freshmen—worry about the end of their first high school grading period. The receipt of grades usually triggers a round of conferences with students and parents and some schedule changes.

The counseling center is as busy in December as one of the suburban malls where the students shop. Ms. Ashton reviews the school's curriculum with an assistant principal, passing on ideas from the students and parents. The return of the PSAT scores also causes a flurry of activity. About this time of year, too, the juniors take part in career exploration workshops and other activities.

According to Dick Clark and the crowd in Times Square, one year ends and another begins on January 1, but no change occurs at the counseling center, where the pace won't let up for months. Deadlines for college applications come and go throughout the winter. Periodically the center holds parent coffees in the evening. The semester ends, requiring more conferences and schedule readjustments as well as signaling the beginning of preregistration counseling for the fall semester. Another major event of the month is the after-school meeting on financial aid, which is always of great concern in this school where a great majority of the students go on for further studies.

By the end of March, minimum competency exams will be given to the sophomores and SRAs to the juniors. The results of these tests, like the results of all the other academic and aptitude assessments made throughout the year, will stimulate visits to the counselors. Events that take place outside the school can also propel people into the center. A television show on incest or teenage suicide, for example, may cause students, their friends, their parents, or their neighbors to contact the counseling center.

April and May largely belong to the juniors, at first glance. A parent night focuses attention on their post-high school plans, and a series of workshops prepares them for applying to colleges. The administration of the college boards and advanced placement exams are particularly time-consuming services. The status of each senior must also be reviewed to ensure that everyone will qualify for graduation. Registration for summer school also takes place throughout this period, a change from the days when students usually took summer school classes to make up for courses they had failed during the regular school year. Ms. Ashton and members of her staff also visit six different junior high schools that feed into Oakton, meeting next year's freshmen and explaining the various educational options open to them.

Paperwork consumes much of Ms. Ashton's time in June. Students take the last of many examinations, and the building quiets down. For two weeks after the end of the semester, the teachers and regular counselors continue to work, winding up one year and planning for the next. Finally, only a few people are left in the building—people like the custodian, the principal, and Mary Ashton. She will have two weeks to tie up loose ends, such as reviewing evaluations from the seniors, and to map out ideas for next year. If she's lucky, she'll have a chance to catch her breath. After all, autumn is just a month away.

CHAPTER 4

ELEMENTARY SCHOOL COUNSELORS: WHAT A DAY!

As the twig...

—A Proverb

The afternoon I visited Houston Elementary School, rain fell heavily, greening the grass and quieting this city neighborhood. A bedraggled robin seeking shelter in a rosebush was the liveliest thing around. The school itself was just as quiet, making me conclude wrongly that classes were over for the day; then a bell rang, and the corridor filled with children ready for the school day and the school week to end. As I entered her office, Ellissia Price—a former American School Counselor's Association "Counselor of the Year"—was giving some final instructions to four students collating an information package. Here, too, all was quiet and calm, a tribute to how well Ms. Price controls the hectic activities of her day.

Her day began with a stop to drop off applications for some of her students to attend a computer camp—the last step after speaking to students, giving out applications, reminding students to return them, and collecting them. Arriving at school, she called the Bureau of Printing and Engraving to confirm arrangements for a field trip the fifth grade class was to make that day.

Ms. Price's own schedule called for visits to three classes in the morning. Counselors rarely have the luxury of doing only what they plan, however, and today's field trip resulted in a slight adjustment. One of the fifth graders—we'll call him Oliver—would not go with his class. Nor would he go to the sixth grade for the morning. His teacher asked Ms. Price for assistance. Oliver agreed to spend the morning with the counselor, an offer she had made with some ambivalence because it would reward his poor behavior with her attention.

Ms. Price knows each of the 366 students in her school, but she sees some more frequently than others. Oliver is one of these. The adults in his life have ignored him, and he feels worthless; he lashes out in school, hoping his poor behavior will win the attention that he feels he does not deserve for himself. This morning, Ms. Price would continue her work with Oliver, adding another block and a little more mortar to his slowly growing sense of responsibility and self-respect. He would also perform some little jobs for her, such as distributing to the teachers the cumulative academic, assessment, and health records of all the students.

Before visiting her first class, Ms. Price also had to consult with a teacher concerning a sixth grader we will call Sherry Finn. One of Ms. Price's personal goals this year is to reduce the absentee rate by five percent. Reaching the goal has required the cooperation of teachers and parents with whom Ms. Price has spoken on the telephone, in her office, and in their homes. Sherry has been a notable part of the attendance concern. Ms. Price has had numerous conversations with her and visited her home, securing the cooperation of her mother in positive ways. Sherry's attendance has improved a hundred percent this year, but the warmth of spring has led to some relapses.

The sixth grade class is one of several that Ms. Price sees regularly. The others she would visit this morning are a special education class for the trainable retarded in the middle grades (ages eight to thirteen) and one for the educable retarded in the same grades. Today all the classes would deal with occupations and careers.

The sixth graders had asked some questions about the appropriateness of different jobs for boys and girls—perhaps it would be more true to say that they had expressed some convictions about the proper place for men and women in the world of work, convictions that have little to do with the reality of our society. Ms. Price used a selection from *Free to Be You and Me* as a springboard for discussion. Although the class seemed to deal only with careers, Ms. Price's ultimate aim was to show that the individual must exercise free and responsible choice in every facet of life.

Group guidance activities such as this cover many subjects, including substance abuse, stranger danger, and child abuse. Sometimes teachers ask Ms. Price to conduct such sessions on a continuing basis. Other times she will suggest holding one, such as when a teacher's evaluations of individual students indicate that a whole class has become unruly. In such a situation, no border can be placed between group guidance and group counseling.

In today's other classes, Ms. Price showed a film about the occupations of workers in a school. She then took the educable class to visit the office and the janitor to reinforce what they had seen so that they could relate the film to the people in their own lives. The trainable students, after seeing the film, drew pictures of people in the various occupations. These different strategies for the three classes are a reminder of the flexibility that Ms. Price must bring to her tasks. She must regularly devise appropriate techniques for dealing with the great variety of concerns of students who fall on every point of the developmental curve, from the slow-learning preschooler to the intellectually superior sixth grader.

At 12:30 on this rainy Friday, Ms. Price went to the kindergarten class and played shape bingo. Once again, an apparently simple activity will do double or even triple duty. The sessions with the kindergarten children and others provide Ms. Price the opportunity of observing the students without being noticed. During them, she can watch how the children interact, identifying those who would benefit from individual counseling. She can also evaluate the students' behavior and skills, using her personal observations to confirm or challenge the results of the formal assessments that she administers. The sessions also serve to increase her visibility so that the students will know her and feel more comfortable about coming to see her. For the children, however, the game is merely fun; they realize neither how important recognizing basic shapes will be to their reading ability nor how much Ms. Price is learning about them.

The afternoon—is it really only afternoon?—began with teacher conferences concerning referrals for special education programs. But once again a student's behavior interrupted Ms. Price's plans. Andrew Kensley, a fourth grader, had threatened another student which triggered reaction from the teacher. Andy, too, was a continuing counselee for Ms. Price. His behavior had worsened recently. It appeared that his stepfather had lost his job and that the family was under great stress. Hoping to have a private conference with Andy's mother, Ms. Price had recently accompanied him home at the end of the school day. Unfortunately, his stepfather was also home that afternoon.

When the last bell rang for the students, Ms. Price still had much to do. For one thing, she was going to talk to me. More typical was her schedule for the previous Friday when she led a session of the Junior Beta Club, a service organization for the sixth graders. Unbeknownst to the students, Ms. Price was developing their decision-making skills by way of a discussion of what to do for the school volunteers at the end of the year. She set the parameters for the gifts—time and money—and led a brainstorming session on gift ideas. Eventually the club members decided to make lollipop corsages similar to a candy corsage one of the students had seen in a florist's window.

Another after-school session that day promised to be more challenging. The parents of three students—two of them under the age of six—were breaking up. Ms. Price was going to meet with the children, just as she would meet with the parents when asked. She would help the youngsters talk about their reaction to the separation by using a feeling board—a large picture that shows children experiencing certain key emotions such as anger, loneliness, fear, and joy. All Ms. Price's training as a counselor would be called upon in learning the meaning behind some of the children's comments.

By the time I left Houston School, the rain had let up, and the water-slick grass looked shellacked in the gray light of the afternoon. A fat worm that had fled its water-soaked hole rewarded the robin for her discomfort during the downpour. The students from Houston were nowhere to be seen. Few of them, probably, remembered their encounters with Ellissia Price that day. Within them, however, the subconscious memory of her lessons would continue to work, helping each of them to consider all the options life offers and to properly value their own worth.

CHAPTER 5

REHABILITATION: FROM ASSESSMENT TO EMPLOYMENT

> Blessed is he who has found his work; let him ask no other
> blessedness.
>
> —Thomas Carlyle

Francis Thomas has been counseling the disabled for many years. Although, like many rehabilitation counselors, he began his career working for a state agency, he is now president of a private rehabilitation firm that provides vocational counseling, alcohol counseling, job placement, and staff development training.

The motto "Above all, do no harm" governs Mr. Thomas's practice; to him, it means that clients should be no worse off at the end of the rehabilitation period than they were before becoming disabled. Among other things, that means they should not suffer a great loss in earning power because of their change of occupation. The case history of one of his recent clients—whose name is not the one used here—shows how Mr. Thomas puts his counseling philosophy into practice. The initial interview might have gone like this:

> Charlie Hartsman eyed the counselor suspiciously. Charlie had collected worker's compensation for a year and a half. Finally, the worker's compensation board had referred him to Francis Thomas for rehabilitation counseling. Mr. Thomas, large of frame and agile of motion, was all that

Charlie would never be again. "Now what?" he thought. Would he soon be able to take charge of his own life again? Was this just a delaying tactic by the board? Was he going to be pushed into a dead-end, minimum-wage job? At least he'd find out soon.

"Good morning, Mr. Hartsman."

"Hi."

"I've looked over your records. I see you injured your back unloading bags of coins for the transit company. Would you like to return to work for them?"

"Yeah. I guess so. You know, I've got some years with them and the retirement and what not. But, you know, they've acted like *I owe them* for messin' up my back, you know what I mean?"

"You feel they haven't been fair to you?"

"Right. Like, I didn't *try* to get hurt, you know what I mean?"

"The way they've handled this, they've put the blame on you."

"Yeah. They're not the only place to work. Still, I do have some years in, like I said."

"Even though you don't like the way the company treated you, you would not mind going back to work for it because of things like your seniority, health insurance, and pension."

"That's right."

"Well, when you were working, did you notice any jobs you'd like?"

"I dunno. Maybe bus checker, the guy who stands at a bus stop and checks what time each bus gets there and how many people are on it and stuff."

The initial interview continues with the counselor moving toward several goals. He must show that he has the client's best interest at heart and establish a counseling relationship. Clients may direct considerable anger and frustration at the counselor during the initial interview or later in their rehabilitation program. By the time clients see a counselor, the reality of their disability has begun to sink in. Because of the length of time that often elapses between the date of the injury and the first session with the counselor, clients may also feel that they have not been treated fairly. On the other hand, some clients may have become adjusted to receiving worker's compensation, which can amount to three-fourths of their previous salary, and see the counselor as a threat to their new way of life.

An additional challenge for the counselor is to get the clients to make their own decisions. The counselor represents authority to many clients, and they are ready to do whatever they are told so they don't lose their benefits. In many cases, the same client will exhibit each of these tendencies—anger, rebellion, and docility—at different times.

After the interview, Mr. Thomas contacted the transit company concerning the bus checker position. He forwarded Charlie's records to them for review. While the company reviewed the case, Mr. Thomas saw his client regularly, providing supportive counseling.

As it turned out, the company would not reemploy Charlie as a checker because the job required being out of doors in all types of weather. It suggested that an indoor job, such as bookkeeping, was a better possibility. Upon receiving this information, Mr. Thomas conducted a counseling session to learn Charlie's reaction to the turn of events. Charlie thought the job might work out, although he would need at least a year of training to qualify for it. In fact, he had wanted to continue his schooling before he went to work, but family circumstances prevented it.

The worker's compensation board would have to approve a training allotment in order for Charlie to attend school, so securing one would be the next order of business. While the board was considering the request, Mr. Thomas explored various school programs with Charlie. Eventually, arrangements were made for him to attend a local business college.

The Hartsman case was more or less on hold during the training period. Francis Thomas continued to provide supportive counseling, seeing his client at least once a month and speaking to him weekly. Mr. Thomas also filed monthly reports to the board. All in all, the case appeared to be heading toward a favorable outcome.

But then some flies showed up in the ointment. Toward the end of the year, the company reported to Mr. Thomas that no position would be available. After another round of discussions, Charlie decided to continue in the training program and earn his associate's degree.

Yet another year passed. At the end of it, Charlie finally went back to work. He still is not working in the accounting department, however, although he has been promised the first job that becomes available.

In some ways, Charlie Hartsman was an easy client to work with. He was not subject to severe depression nor did he become dependent on drugs or alcohol after his injury. Furthermore, he was willing to work indoors at a desk job, working conditions that appear intolerable to many of the formerly active disabled. He also had an aptitude for accounting and wanted to go back to school. Still, the case took more than three years to resolve, hardly a short time in a person's life.

At the end of those three years, however, Francis Thomas had more than the satisfaction of knowing that he had "done no harm." He had taken an unskilled client with a back injury and returned him to the labor force with the promise of a good career in a field full of opportunities for professional advancement.

CHAPTER 6

MENTAL HEALTH COUNSELING

Mental health counseling is a specialty that includes many kinds of counselors, from marriage and family specialists to those who counsel individuals or groups. Licensing of counselors in many states brought recognition and enabled counselors to do much needed work with clients.

Managed care concepts are making an impact on behavioral care, now, with the effect of tightening health care budgets everywhere in an effort to contain costs for employers, insurance companies, and government agencies. The best way to find out about mental health counseling is to ask some counselors who have worked full time in the field.

Dr. Joseph Scalise is a counselor in Georgia. In addition to his counseling work, he's been active in promoting the licensing of counselors through state legislation, which passed in Georgia, giving needed recognition to mental health counseling as a specialty.

Q: Why did you choose the private practice of counseling?

A: After I finished my doctoral degree I worked at the university for about ten years. I was chairman of the counseling department. I always maintained a private practice; it was something I liked to do. Full-time private practice gives me the opportunity to set my own hours and be in charge of my own fate.

Q: What is your day like?

A: In a typical day I see several kind of clients—individuals, couples, or families. I have progress notes to dictate and forms to fill out, treatment plans, specifically. We have an office manager and staff here who handle all the insurance filing, but I also do the work of trying to get additional sessions approved by insurance companies, if necessary. I also do some writing each week for publication.

Q: How do clients find your practice?

A: That's one of the things that's not taught very well in training programs. It's difficult for therapists to realize that this is a business. When you're just getting started you have to work with other therapists, physicians, lawyers, and agencies that might be in a position to refer clients to you, etc. But over the long-term, the best referral source are the people that you work with, your satisfied customers. Place an ad in the phone book, a note in the (news)paper, and send out cards to other practitioners, doctors, and hospitals. Also find out what associations are active in the community and get involved with other professionals.

Q: What do you envision for counselors entering the field?

A: If people are flexible in terms of where they want to live or work, that can make a difference. Some of the more rural areas are screaming for help. Also if they find a niche, something that they do well, their special skills will be easier to market.

Q: What are some good specialties to consider?

A: One thing people do a lot of training in now is group work. To use the language of managed care, that's a "cost-effective treatment modality." They need to diversify, too. They may need to consult with business and industry, as to the impact of mental health problems on their employees. It's pretty obvious that if a worker's child is having trouble in school or trouble with drugs, the employee is not going to be as productive. It is your job to show them how they can have happier and more loyal employees by providing certain services.

Q: What would be a standard work load for a private practice?

A: Anywhere from 20 to 30 hours of client contact. That might include couples or families. Additional time is needed with paperwork, protocols, follow-up, and so on.

Q: What is the ideal education for the counselor?

A: Much depends on the individual, where they live and if they're able to move or are restricted. Before choosing a school, they need to talk to people in the field, and people who've recently graduated from universities they're able to attend. They need to examine the training program to see how much experience, practicum, or internship is in the program. The more experience the better.

Q: What is the difference between a mental health counselor and a psychiatrist?

A: One of the most obvious differences is that a psychiatrist is a medical doctor and can prescribe medication. With the advent of managed care, they're being put in the position of having to do medication work almost exclusively, whereas counselors, social workers, and others provide additional types of therapy.

Q: What's the good side of licensure?

A: Well, I think it's given people credibility. In the past when you weren't licensed by the state, consumers looked at you as some kind of second-class citizen.

Linda Lawless, LMCH, LMFT (Licensed Marriage and Family Therapist) lives in Boston, Massachusetts, where she has a private practice. She has taught at Fitchburg State College and Leslie College. Before moving East, she spent six years in California as a full-time counselor. She has developed some specialties that drive her marketing effort as a counselor in private practice.

Q: What options are available in mental health counseling, with the cost pressures of managed care today?

A: There are going to be the people who will work in managed care and with that short-term model. And there will be people who will want to do the long-term work and will design programs that are market favorable, like stress-reduction programs, helping in schools, and helping with businesses. So clinicians are not only going to be good clinicians, they're going to have to be good businesspeople, and get more creative in the ways they package and market their services to the marketplace.

Q: Are there any models for that?

A: One woman colleague of mine specializes in stepparenting, so when anyone has stepparenting issues, they go to her. She sees individuals and groups. That's become her niche. Others have gone into the mediation arena.

Q: Are you a full-time counselor now?

A: When I first came to Massachusetts I went into teaching. I was a full-time counselor in California for six years. I'm part-time in counseling now. I also teach and consult.

Q: What kinds of problems do you see, and what does success look like?

A: I truly enjoy the work. "Success" is a client who comes in with many life problems and terminates successfully, feeling they can control their situation. Surprisingly, I get letters from folks I saw years ago, telling me they got married or had children; that's really nice.

Q: Do you have specialties?

A: Now I'm specializing in women and power, women and success, and couples.

Q: Can you describe that?

A: I get women who are having some type of difficulty in their primary relationships, or women who have been abused—physical abuse as well as psychological abuse. I help them learn how to take care of themselves, set limits, increase their self-esteem, and choose relationships that are nurturing rather than destructive. For women and success issues, I advise them that they have to create their own definition of success, and not just buy one out of the media. They have to stand behind it and honor it, if that means going back to school, changing jobs, or choosing to not have children; these are tough stances for women to take. For couples, communication is the primary tool. It can go in one of two directions, either toward strengthening the relationship or toward a separation—but separating in a way that isn't emotionally devastating, so that they can come out of it feeling stronger.

Q: What do new counselors need to know about mental health counseling?

A: They need to enjoy the work and keep growing themselves. Anybody in private practice needs to be in supervision. I have a therapist that I meet with, along with two or three other clinicians every month, and we talk about cases we feel we're stuck on or lack clarity in. We also talk about our own personal issues that are touched by various clients. I think these meetings are absolutely necessary, so that you're not working out your personal issues during a client's hour.

CHAPTER 7

SCHOOL COUNSELORS:
FACTS AND FIGURES

OTHER JOB TITLES

Guidance counselor, adjustment counselor, crisis resource teacher, career guidance counselor, guidance director, learning specialist, middle school/junior high school counselor, elementary school counselor, intervention specialist, child development specialist.

GOALS AND DUTIES

School counselors help students understand themselves, clarify the opportunities available to them, and reach their goals.

School counselors have at least seven general duties: counseling students or others; consulting with parents, teachers, administrators, and other student personnel workers such as school psychologists and social workers; appraising the abilities and aptitudes of students through tests and other procedures; informing students and others concerning the school's programs, other educational programs, employment opportunities, and the availability of social services; referring students or other counselees to more specialized avenues of counseling or treatment; administering the guidance program; and conducting research or continuing their own education.

The following services are offered by a typical guidance department: orientation of new students; assignment of students to classes; provision of information and counseling for students individually and in groups concerning study skills, educational plans, career plans, employment opportunities, financial aid, behavioral difficulties, social development, and personal problems; consultation with administrators, teachers, and parents concerning the educational, vocational, social, and personal development of individual students and the student body as a whole; training of administrators, teachers, and parents to work with students more effectively; scheduling, administering, and explaining the results of aptitude, ability, and interest tests for individuals and groups; keeping records of students' academic work, extracurricular activities, goals, accomplishments, attendance, and reasons for leaving school; and placement of students in employment in or outside the school.

The amount of time an individual counselor spends on any single activity is subject to enormous variation, largely because of administrative decisions made by the school principal or school board. In the words of Dr. Edwin L. Herr, testifying before the U.S. Senate, "What school counselors do is ultimately shaped by the characteristics of the local school districts in which they are employed." Counselors would prefer to spend most of their time in consultant and counselor roles, with the balance spent on research and the administration of the guidance program.

Counselors in the schools are not the only ones who provide pupil services. Other members of the pupil services team may include a psychologist, social worker, nurse, and attendance officer. Several of these occupations are discussed in the chapter on other counseling-related occupations. Admissions, housing, student activities, financial aid, and religious activities also fall under pupil services. The duties of a counselor depend in part on how a school district uses these other personnel.

The kind of work counselors do in the schools also depends in part on the grade of the students served: secondary, elementary, or middle and junior high school students.

SECONDARY SCHOOL COUNSELORS

According to the College Entrance Examination Board's Commission on Precollege Guidance and Counseling, "The school counselor should be first and foremost an educator, supporting students in their progress through the school and serving as a crucial resource for the academic program." Secondary school counselors generally deal with four types of subjects or concerns: educational, vocational, social, and personal.

Educational concerns range from freshman orientation (an information function), to administering entrance examinations (an appraisal function), to helping a student sort out the advantages and disadvantages of various postsecondary programs (a counseling function). Personal concerns might be dealt with through a group guidance arrangement (such as a workshop on time management and study skills) or either individual or group counseling (such as a group of the friends of a student who committed suicide).

The following role statement for secondary school counselors from the American School Counselor Association has been revised, but it still captures the counselor's duties:

- Organize and implement through interested teachers guidance curricula interventions that focus upon important developmental concerns of adolescents (identity, career choice and planning, social relationships, and so forth).

- Organize and make available comprehensive information systems (print, computer-based, audiovisual) necessary for educational-vocational planning and decision making.
- Assist students with assessment of personal characteristics (e.g., competencies, interests, aptitudes, needs, career maturity) for personal use in such areas as course selection, post-high school planning, and career choices.
- Provide remedial interventions or alternative programs for those students showing in-school adjustment problems, vocational immaturity, or general negative attitudes toward personal growth.

In a single week's work, a secondary school counselor might have a conference with several teachers concerning a student's behavior, process an application for a student's part-time job, meet with the principals of the high school and middle school to make plans for the orientation of next year's freshmen, consult with a parent about a student's adjustment to a new family situation, help a student understand the results of an aptitude test, lead a group session for the friends of a student who committed suicide, administer an academic achievement test to the sophomore class, help a group of seniors decide which colleges to apply for, and show some juniors how to use a computer terminal to find out about different careers.

Typically, of course, the work would be far less varied. In many schools, for example, a counselor would work with only one class rather than all four. In others, a counselor will work with the ninth and eleventh grades one year and the tenth and twelfth grades the next, an arrangement that gives students the advantage of continuity and counselors the advantage of variety.

Not all counselors find their jobs so multifaceted. Some complain that they are little more than office clerks handling academic transcripts, schedule changes, school applications, attendance registers, and administrative duties. Surveys have found that many secondary school counselors spend one-third to two-thirds of their time on relatively routine paperwork or registration activities.

ELEMENTARY SCHOOL COUNSELORS

Elementary school counselors report doing more counseling and more consulting with teachers, administrators, and parents than secondary school counselors do. As much as 80 percent of the elementary school counselor's time may be spent in these activities, with about half that time spent with students and much of the rest with teachers. Educational and vocational concerns take up relatively little of the elementary school counselor's time, while social and personal concerns take relatively more than is the case in secondary schools. In addition, the techniques of counseling an elementary school pupil differ markedly from those used with adolescents. For example, play, drawing, and storytelling may be utilized simply to learn the nature of the pupil's concern.

The following role statement from the American School Counselor Association sums up the duties of elementary school counselors:

- Provide in-service training to teachers to assist them with planning and implementing guidance interventions for young children (preschool to third grade) in order to maximize developmental benefits (self-esteem, personal relationship, positive school attitudes, and so forth) in the hope of preventing serious problems or minimizing the size of such problems if and when they do occur.
- Provide consultations for teachers who need help understanding and incorporating developmental concepts in teacher content as well as support for building a healthy classroom environment.

- Accommodate parents who need assistance with understanding normal child growth and development and their role in encouraging their child to learn as well as improving family communication skills.
- Cooperate with other school staff in the early identification, remediation, or referral of children with developmental deficiencies or handicaps.
- As children reach the upper elementary grades, effort is directed through the curriculum toward increasing student awareness of the relationship between school and work, especially the impact of educational choices on one's lifestyle and career development.

MIDDLE AND JUNIOR HIGH SCHOOL COUNSELORS

Students in middle and junior high schools are often spoken of as *transescent,* or in transition from childhood to adolescence. The duties of counselors who work in these schools, therefore, might be expected to resemble a cross between the duties of elementary school and secondary school counselors. They do.

Junior high school counselors in one study reported spending 85 percent of their time counseling. Counselors in another study reported spending 50 to 60 percent of their time counseling students in regard to improving interpersonal relationships, values clarification, crises such as death and divorce, and the physical, emotional, and other changes of puberty. Counselors in this study also reported spending 10 to 25 percent of their time coordinating services to the student, 10 to 20 percent as consultants working with teachers or other adults who deal with the students, and 2 to 33 percent as curriculum specialists conducting in-service training, group guidance for students on subjects such as human sexuality or career education, and parent education programs.

The American School Counselor Association has developed the following role statement for middle and junior high school counselors:

- Concentrate efforts...to smooth the transition of the student from the [lower school to the middle or junior high school].
- Identify, encourage, and support teachers (through in-service training, consultation, and coteaching) who are interested in incorporating developmental units in [their curriculums].
- Organize and implement a career guidance program that includes an assessment of [each student's] career maturity and career-planning status; easy access to relevant career information; and assistance with processing data for personal use in schoolwork-related decision making.

EMPLOYMENT AND OUTLOOK

According to the U.S. Center for Education Statistics, there were approximately 84,958 guidance counselors in the public schools in 1994. According to many experts, the job market is currently good for prospective counselors. The outlook for the future is also promising, because of an expected increase in secondary school enrollment.

Although the job outlook for school counselors differs greatly by the educational level of the students served, the data available do not permit such an analysis. It is possible, however, to project the demand for school counselors in general and then comment on probable trends at the different levels. The demand for counselors is determined by three factors: the number of students, the ratio of counselors to students, and the number of working counselors who leave the occupation.

In the fall of 1994, there were more than forty-four million students in public elementary and secondary schools, according to the U.S. Department of Education. These schools employed about 85,000 counselors, or about 1 counselor for every 585 students; most private high schools also employ counselors. The Department projects a public school enrollment of over forty-seven million in the year 2000. To maintain the same ratio of counselors to students, therefore, would require an additional 13,500 counselors, an increase of 16 percent. Population projections from the Bureau of the Census indicate little change between 1997 and 2000. Those projections do make clear, however, that increased immigration could push the demand for more counselors. Demand would also be higher if schools try to reduce the ratio of counselors to students, as was the trend in the first half of the 1980s.

Important as growth can be to an occupation, it usually accounts for only a small fraction of total openings. This is certainly the case in counseling. Most jobs become available because of turnover, which occurs when people in an occupation leave it. According to the U.S. Department of Labor, the need for replacement counselors will increase significantly through the year 2000, resulting from the large number of counselors who will retire in the near future.

The supply of people to fill these openings comes from two sources: experienced counselors not currently in the occupation and new recipients of master's degrees. People in the field say that shortages are likely and that they might even be severe in states or school districts that are growing rapidly or that are reducing their student-counselor ratios. The available data generally support this view, although difficulties with classification make only rough comparisons possible.

While firm projections of the demand for counselors by grade level are not possible, certain trends can be identified. High school enrollments are projected to rise about 22 percent from 1996 to 2006 by the National Center for Education Statistics. Such a rise would increase employment of counselors by a similar percentage. Employment would rise more quickly if counselor-student ratios are reduced. This is not likely in the near future, however. In fact, although some school districts have far too many students per counselor and some rural students have no access to a counselor at all, the ratio of high school counselors to high school students is fairly close to the 1 to 250 sought. The situation would change, of course, if money were actually provided to conduct the kinds of programs that are sometimes recommended to combat alcohol and drug abuse, teenage pregnancies, and other problems faced by young people. Turnover among high school counselors will, however, provide thousands of openings.

Elementary enrollments are projected to rise only 4 percent. The employment of elementary school counselors is likely to rise faster than this, however. The number of elementary school counselors is far below the recommended level, a ratio of one counselor to five hundred students. There is, therefore, considerable room for growth in the occupation simply to achieve the recommended ratio. Many school districts and several states have recently begun to employ counselors in the elementary schools. But actual growth is still likely to be far slower than potential growth since it is closely tied to tax revenues and expenditures for public schools. In all probability, therefore, growth will be substantial in school districts committed to elementary school guidance programs and minimal in school districts that do not stress such activities.

SALARY, OTHER BENEFITS, AND WORKING CONDITIONS

According to the Educational Research Service, the average salary for school counselors was $38,000 a year in 1990. In 1996, salaries ranged from a low of about $24,000 to a high of more than $50,000. Counselors, therefore, earn somewhat more than classroom teachers, in part because they must have more education and experience to qualify for entry-level positions. They enjoy the usual fringe benefits of teachers, such as health insurance and pension plans.

Generally, the work year for school counselors either matches the school year or runs a month longer, starting two weeks before the beginning of the first term and finishing two weeks after the end of the last term. Although work hours conform to the school day, more or less, counselors often conduct special programs or hold office hours in the evening for students or parents who want to drop by.

Secondary school counselors usually have offices that ensure privacy. Counselors in elementary schools built before guidance programs for the lower grades originated may have makeshift office space. Clerical assistance is inadequate for some counselors.

ENTRY REQUIREMENTS AND CAREER LADDER

The requirements for certification as a school counselor are established independently by each state; in other words, this meat loaf has fifty recipes. A master's degree in counseling or guidance is almost universally a condition of employment. More than three hundred graduate schools have programs that prepare counselors with titles such as guidance, counseling, elementary school guidance, and pupil personnel services. They are usually in the counselor education department of a school of education. The degree entails from thirty to sixty semester hours of course work; fifteen hours in a semester is considered a full schedule. A practicum lasting one hundred to six hundred hours of contact with clients may also be compulsory. Most states also require one to three years of teaching experience, although several now allow the substitution of counseling experience for teaching experience. If a state calls for teaching experience, a prospective counselor must first qualify for teacher certification, which usually requires a set number of education courses taken as an undergraduate or in graduate school and a supervised teaching practicum. Provisional certification may be available for counselors who have not completed their graduate programs. Certification granted by one state will probably not be automatically recognized by another state. A list of state accrediting agencies that can provide detailed information appears in Appendix C.

Counselors are at the top of their profession. They may change occupations, however, to increase their earnings, gain more administrative responsibility, or be free to do more specialized work. Counselors can become directors of guidance, counseling, or student personnel services or school administrators; additional graduate-school work in school administration is usually required. Counselors can become professors in counselor education programs; a doctorate is usually required. They may enter private practice, which might require additional certification. And they may become school psychologists or enter related occupations; again, additional education, possibly including a doctorate, is usually mandatory. A survey of graduates of a National Defense Education Act institute for elementary school counselors showed that a few were still counselors thirteen years later, but others had become administrators, social workers, counselors in nonelementary school settings, professors in counselor education programs, or psychological examiners. Some had returned to teaching. Other surveys confirm these findings.

More information about this occupation is available from the associations and in the books and journals listed in Appendixes A and B. You should also contact the department of education or public instruction in your state to learn the certification requirements. State affiliates of national associations such as the American Counseling Association and the National Education Association also may have useful information.

A NOTE ON INDEPENDENT
EDUCATIONAL CONSULTANTS

Some counselors have established private practices that focus on educational placements for high school or college students or students in need of special education. Private practice for this type of counseling is fairly uncommon, but this specialty is growing. Independent advisors now number about 1,000, up 300 percent from 1980. People in private practice usually work alone but may have two or three associates, each of whom has a specialty. For example, one associate might have experience teaching in Europe and be familiar with educational placement overseas; another might concentrate on students who need special education.

Often a private educational counselor acts as a consultant to a mental health counselor or psychiatrist who is seeking an educational program for a client. Other clients seek more individual attention than can be provided by a high school counselor. The educational counselor meets with the client and parents, collects information on the client's educational history, aptitudes, financial resources, and educational goals, and tries to make an optimum placement.

Independent educational counselors are not burdened by the administrative duties of school counselors, but school counselors are not burdened with hiring office personnel and collecting fees. Typically, independent counselors have ten to fifteen years' experience before entering private practice. Their earnings are comparable to those of school counselors.

More information, specifically a directory of members, is available from the Independent Educational Consultants Association, 4085 Chain Bridge Road, Suite 401, Fairfax, Virginia, 22030–4106, (703) 591–4850.

CHAPTER 8

MENTAL HEALTH COUNSELORS: FACTS AND FIGURES

OTHER JOB TITLES

Marriage counselor; family therapist; marriage, family, and divorce counselor; community agency counselor.

GOALS AND DUTIES

Mental health counselors assist people in coping with problems. The range of goals and duties for these counselors matches the complete range for all counselors. The client's concerns can range from a child's difficulties in adjusting to a divorce to an older person's anxiety about entering a nursing home. Alcohol and drug abuse, family conflicts, child and spouse abuse, difficulty at work, criminal behavior, and changes in family status are among the problems encountered. Besides providing individual and group counseling, these counselors coordinate treatment plans, administer programs to improve mental health conditions in the community, and intervene in crisis situations.

EMPLOYMENT AND OUTLOOK

Employment probably exceeds fifty thousand, indicating that no counseling specialty has more practitioners. That figure is only an educated guess, however, derived from taking the number of people identified as counselors in one federal survey (206,000) and subtracting from it the probable numbers of school, rehabilitation, employment, and college counselors. It is comparable to rough estimates made by the American Counseling Association, using the membership of its mental health division as a foundation. There are 9,000 mental health counselors in the American Mental Health Counselors Association. Marriage and family therapy has grown rapidly. One group, the International Association of Marriage and Family Counselors (IAMFC), grew from 140 members in 1986 to 8,000 members ten years later, when it was the fastest-growing association in the behavioral sciences, according to the *Journal of Counseling & Development* (November/December 1995, p. 155).

The ways used to count the number of people who work in an occupation break down fairly completely for this one. The difficulty, as usual, is lack of agreement as to who works in the occupation. Among those who could be counted as mental health counselors are ministers, priests, and rabbis, who spend much of their time counseling members of their congregations, and people with doctorates in psychology who would usually be considered psychologists. Marriage and family therapists, another closely related occupation, may also be counted among mental health counselors by some; they number twelve thousand or more.

Employers of mental health counselors include mental health clinics, educational institutions, community agencies, social service agencies, prisons, group homes, drug rehabilitation programs, and health maintenance organizations. The National Institutes of Health surveys employment in psychiatric hospitals, clinics, and other facilities. Because employers rarely distinguish between psychologists and counselors, the survey does not provide data for counselors. Thousands of mental health counselors work in private practice. In addition, many counselor educators and counselors employed by community agencies have part-time private practices.

More than half the graduates of counselor education programs now go into community and agency work. Most say, however, that the total number of graduates with this specialty is about the same as the number of positions available, in part because of a drop in the number of graduates. Others say that the field is still competitive. In all probability, the success of graduates in finding positions depends in part on the reputation of the school they attend and their willingness to relocate.

This occupation is expected to grow faster than average over the next ten years. The major uncertainty in determining the rate of growth is related to the issue of third-party payment. Over the past few years, many insurance plans have reduced the amount of money they will pay for mental health services, and this has acted as a brake on the growth of mental health occupations. At the same time, however, insurers have begun to authorize the payment of counselors for services once performed by psychologists. Should this trend continue, the employment of counselors will continue to grow. The need for these services is clearly expanding, although the willingness of insurance companies to pay for them might not.

SALARY, OTHER BENEFITS, AND WORKING CONDITIONS

The range of salaries naturally matches the range of employers. The earnings of almost all mental health counselors falls within the $11,000 to $50,000 range. Earnings of counselors in private practice depend largely on the number of hours worked. Typically, the hourly fee charged by counselors in private practice in 1990 was between $40 and $100 for individual counseling and $25 to $70 for group sessions. The number of sessions held per week varied so widely that the average would not be representative.

Mental health counselors employed by public agencies receive the same fringe benefits as other government workers, including group health insurance, retirement plans, and sick leave. Benefits at community agencies are usually comparable. Counselors in private practice are responsible for their own medical insurance, liability insurance, and pensions.

ENTRY REQUIREMENTS AND CAREER LADDER

The usual educational requirement is a master's degree in counseling for a community or agency setting. Graduates of longer programs that require three hundred or more hours of supervised counseling experience are preferred. These positions are also held by graduates of master's, doctorate, and certificate programs in marriage and family therapy, psychology, or social work.

Advancement can take the form of increased specialization in a particular type of counseling—such as spouse abuse—or increased administrative duties in an agency.

Certification and licensure for counselors is discussed in the chapter on current issues; the situation is changing rapidly. At the moment, certification for counselors in these positions is granted by several bodies.

The National Board for Certified Counselors administers a specialized certification procedure for each state and grants a generic certification. Many certified counselors are affiliated with the American Counseling Association, 5999 Stevenson Avenue, Alexandria, Virginia 22304, (703) 823-9800, including the American Mental Health Counselors Association.

The American Association of Sex Educators, Counselors, and Therapists (435 North Michigan Avenue, Suite 1717, Chicago, Illinois 60611) has separate certification requirements for sex counselors and sex therapists as well as educators and supervisors.

A state license to practice is required in about 40 states, with the number increasing. Marriage and family therapists must be licensed in about 20 states. Addresses for both kinds of licensing boards are in Appendix C. All the states license psychologists; the American Psychological Association (750 First Street, NE, Washington, D.C., 20002) can provide a list of addresses.

More information about mental health counselors is available from many of the agencies and associations listed in Appendix A as well as in most general books on counseling. Registers of certified or licensed counselors and listings in the classified telephone directory can lead you to practicing counselors with whom you can discuss the occupation.

CHAPTER 9

REHABILITATION COUNSELORS: FACTS AND FIGURES

OTHER JOB TITLES

Vocational rehabilitation counselor.

GOALS AND DUTIES

Rehabilitation counselors assist the disabled in becoming employed or leading fuller lives.

Rehabilitation counselors interview a client and administer tests to determine a plan of services to provide. They identify suitable occupations for the client. They provide vocational counseling, including identifying suitable occupations, and assist clients in adjusting to their disabilities, a task that can require the total range of a counselor's skills. Job placement—which may depend on modifications suggested by the counselor—is the ultimate goal for the majority of clients. Related duties include case management, the coordination of vocational, medical, and psychological services, provision of financial maintenance, and professional development.

Individual counselors may specialize on a single facet of the occupation, such as cultivating good relations with potential employers, or on a single disability.

Rehabilitation services are provided by state agencies to the deaf, blind, mobility impaired, emotionally disabled, and mentally retarded. Government programs also provide rehabilitation counseling for recovering alcoholics, drug addicts, and prisoners. Recipients of worker's compensation also qualify for rehabilitation services in many states. Typically, these services are provided by private companies or private practitioners who are paid by insurance companies.

A counselor's case load can range from 20 to 150 clients; some cases can be closed in three months or less like Charlie Hartsman's, but more than 40 percent take more than a year to resolve. Clients may be referred to the counselor by hospitals, doctors, educational institutions, insurance companies, and worker's compensation boards.

Duties of counselors differ somewhat depending on whether they work for a government agency or a private firm. For example, more than 40 percent of the clients of rehabilitation counselors are mentally ill or retarded; generally, however, only counselors with state agencies are likely to have clients with these conditions. The 20 percent or so of clients suffering from impaired use of a limb or amputation, however, are more likely to receive counseling through an insurance or worker's compensation program. Counselors in public agencies often deal with more severe handicaps and disabilities and have larger case loads. They must also seek remedies for barriers to employment of the handicapped and disabled such as inaccessibility to wheelchairs.

EMPLOYMENT AND OUTLOOK

The employment of rehabilitation counselors exceeds twenty thousand. Counselors employed by the state work in agencies for the handicapped or disabled, mental health institutions, hospitals, schools, and penal institutions. About half the counselors work in the private sector. Private firms vary widely in size, ranging from one-person operations to companies that employ sixty or more full-time counselors. The Department of Veterans Affairs employs numerous counselors, classified as counseling psychologists. The total number of certified rehabilition counselors reached 13,594 in 1996, according to the Commission on Rehabilitation Counselor Certification (CRCC).

Overall, this occupation has recently been growing at a rapid rate, almost all of it in the private sector. This private-sector growth is expected to continue, along with slight growth in state agencies in some regions. Many counselors might begin their careers in the public sector and move to private practice.

Employment growth in private companies depends on state laws. Typically, when a state first makes rehabilitation a mandatory part of its worker's compensation laws, employment of rehabilitation counselors in private companies grows very rapidly. Some contraction may then take place as the laws are modified. Eventually, a slow but steady rate of growth is attained.

The future is also bright, according to numerous experts. Besides openings from continued growth, the need to replace counselors who leave the occupation will account for many jobs. This occupation has a surprisingly high turnover rate, especially considering the extensive education required. Much of the turnover, according to several people in the field, results from the ability of counselors to move to more attractive positions with other agencies or to become administrators. The shortage of fully qualified counselors and necessity of hiring people with only a bachelor's degree also explains some of the turnover, however. Some of these people probably are dissatisfied with their jobs because they failed to investigate the nature of the work beforehand. It is very important to speak to practitioners and work in paraprofessional or other capacities at least for a short time before committing to an occupation.

The National Council on Rehabilitation Education surveys rehabilitation programs in colleges and universities every couple of years. In the early 1990s, virtually all who completed a graduate program in rehabilitation went to work in the field. The number of graduates declined compared to the previous two-year period, perhaps because of fears that federal support for students in these programs would be cut—a fear that still concerns educators. Federal aid is still generally available for graduate study in rehabilitation, and many schools have affirmative recruitment policies.

About one-third of these graduates went to work in the private sector. In all likelihood, many of the recent graduates who went to work for public agencies will transfer to the private sector after gaining more experience, thus contributing to the apparently high turnover rate discussed above. The report also found that 75 percent of the graduates of undergraduate programs in rehabilitation services were working in the field, an extremely high percentage.

SALARY, OTHER BENEFITS, AND WORKING CONDITIONS

In 1996, annual salaries in the private sector are in the $26,000 to $38,000 range, with top salaries of more than $100,000 possible. The hourly rate of compensation for a counselor in private practice is approximately $55 to $85.

Beginning salaries in state agencies averaged less than in the private sector. The average salary in state agencies for experienced counselors was about $29,000 in the early 1990s, but the range was very wide, going from $14,460 to $65,750. Generally, most practicing counselors were earning from the mid-twenties to the low-forties.

Fringe benefits enjoyed by counselors depend on their employer. Counselors with state agencies and most private companies enjoy the usual benefits, such as paid vacations, health insurance, and pension plans. Private agencies may also provide an automobile for counselors.

Rehabilitation counselors perform most of their duties in regular offices. They must also visit employers, however, both to arrange placements and to follow up on the placement of clients.

ENTRY REQUIREMENTS AND CAREER LADDER

States show some variety in hiring requirements. Most agencies require either a bachelor's degree and two years of experience or a master's degree in rehabilitation counseling and no experience. Some state agencies hire inexperienced holders of bachelor's degrees, while other agencies require that even master's degree holders have work experience.

Private companies have the same hiring standards as state agencies, which is to say that holders of a master's degree in rehabilitation counseling are preferred but that other people are also sometimes hired. Increasingly, however, employers seek certified counselors, and a master's degree is a prerequisite.

A degree in rehabilitation counseling includes courses on the principles of rehabilitation, the psychosocial effects of disability, counseling techniques, and assessment. There are about eighty graduate programs for rehabilitation counseling and around fifteen undergraduate programs in rehabilitation services; most are either separate departments or part of a counselor education department in a school of education. More than seventy programs are accredited by the Foundation on Rehabilitation Education; about twice as many exist altogether.

The large number of rehabilitation counselors who have been certified indicates its desirability. Certification of counselors is granted by the Foundation for Rehabilitation Counseling Education and Research, 1835 Rohlwing Road, Rolling Meadows, Illinois 60008, (847) 394-1785. A master's degree in rehabilitation counseling granted by a program accredited by the Foundation on Rehabilitation Education and completion of an internship supervised by a certified rehabilitation counselor qualifies an individual in one category of certification while other categories require one to seven years of work experience, depending on the kind of education a person has. The Foundation can provide specific information.

Advancement for counselors is usually a matter of promotion within the same agency or company. In fact, most state agencies do not hire above the entry level, preferring to promote from within. Some hiring at the mid-level does take place among private companies. Advancement may mean increased specialization in a particular aspect of rehabilitation, concentration on a particular form of disability, or increased administrative duties.

For more information about this occupation, contact state agencies that employ rehabilitation counselors. Among the directories that can be used to find individual counselors to speak to concerning the occupation are local guides to social and welfare service agencies and lists of registered counselors. The heading "rehabilitation services" is used in the classified telephone directory. Other relevant guides are listed in Appendix B.

CHAPTER 10

COLLEGE COUNSELORS AND STUDENT AFFAIRS ADMINISTRATORS: FACTS AND FIGURES

OTHER JOB TITLES

Staff counselor, career counselor, crisis center coordinator, human development counselor, dean of students, vice-president for student affairs, vice-chancellor for academic affairs, director of student housing, director of alumni affairs, director of student counseling and placement, director of residence life, residence hall counselor, director of religious activities, student union director, foreign student advisor, veterans coordinator, student health services director, student organization advisor, advisor to fraternities and sororities organizations, recreation specialist, athletic director, financial aid administrator, director of admissions, registrar.

GOALS AND DUTIES

College counselors assist all students in identifying and reaching their academic, personal, and vocational goals.

The difficulty in describing the work of high school counselors is that the single job title covers so many duties. The difficulty with college positions is quite the opposite; as the list on the previous page shows, postsecondary schools often use specialized titles and have separate departments for each of the services provided by guidance and counseling offices in high schools. In other cases, however, a person will wear several hats; for example, the financial aid administrator will also be the registrar, dean of students, or admissions officer.

The following services frequently come under the heading of student affairs:

- Academic counseling
- Financial aid counseling and administration
- Health services administration and counseling
- Coordination of student activities, including athletics
- Facilities management
- Vocational/career assessment and counseling
- Placement services
- Psychological counseling

A survey of chief student affairs officers conducted by Daniel Robinson for the National Association of Student Personnel Administrators found that more than 80 percent of them were responsible for the counseling center, housing, career planning and placement, student health, student life, and the student union (a building in which extracurricular activities are held). Twenty percent were even responsible for security.

Each service involves a constellation of activities. For example, workers in a career planning and placement center may schedule interviews, distribute employment information, maintain a career and employer library, administer aptitude tests, run workshops on job-finding skills, cultivate contacts with potential employers, and, in addition to providing career counseling, perform academic counseling.

Some of these activities may seem remote from counseling, but the separation is often more apparent than real. Housing, for example, may include the training of resident advisors, who act as a first link in a counseling chain. Other activities—those related to a university counseling center, for example—are more obviously counseling activities. Furthermore, people in administrative positions often have additional duties involving counseling; for example, almost all of the career planning and placement directors who responded to a College Placement Council survey several years ago said that they performed personal counseling in addition to their career planning and placement activities. In fact, however, many postsecondary positions do require organizational and administrative skills as well as counseling skills.

Surveys of counselors in particular (rather than student affairs workers in general) have found that they spend the majority of their time on educational counseling and advisement. Other activities included conferring with students on probation, developing informative material on counseling-related topics, and planning orientation programs for new students. Providing services for students who intend to transfer was a significant activity for counselors in community colleges; these services include seminars, group meetings, campus visits, and college days. Counselors were assigned to veterans offices, handicapped programs, women's centers, career counseling centers, and financial aid offices where they might be responsible for the placement of students in work study programs as well as in the administration of loans and scholarships.

A survey of community college counselors in New Jersey found that they spent 64 percent of their time on individual or personal counseling and advisement; 15 percent of their time was taken up with administrative duties; and the rest of their time was divided among such activities as committee work, testing, group advising, teaching, and research.

EMPLOYMENT AND OUTLOOK

What cannot be defined can hardly be counted. The number of workers in student affairs depends on which occupations are included in the group. Registrars, for example, are certainly not counselors, although they do work in student affairs. Variation in size among institutions contributes to the uncertainty. At a very small school, a single person might administer both admissions and financial aid programs while a large school could have a dozen professionals in the placement office alone. The average counseling center in a community college employs two professional counselors.

Although precise employment data are unavailable, the following numbers will give a rough indication of the size of these occupations. The number of postsecondary institutions gives a fixed point of departure; according to the U.S. Department of Education, there are approximately 4,000 public and private universities, colleges, and two-year institutions. Almost all have a placement office and other student affairs workers with some of the job titles listed. On large campuses, the director of student affairs may supervise fifty to a hundred professionals. Employment of fifty-five thousand or so is probable, according to several people in the field. Employment for particular specialties, according to the National Association of Student Personnel Administrators, is given in the following tabulation of mean salaries. For example, while only sixteen hundred people are listed for financial aid administration, the actual number of professionals working in financial aid could easily be double or triple the figure, according to a survey conducted by the National Association of Student Financial Affairs Administrators.

Despite the absence of a firm employment count, there is surprising agreement on the outlook for student affairs professionals:

because employment is tied to enrollment and no growth in enroll-ment is expected, employment should remain stable. The U.S. Department of Education actually projects declines in college enrollment through 1997; although these projections are based on the sharp decline in the college-age population that is now occur-ring, it should be noted that enrollment has so far changed very lit-tle. At any rate, there will be numerous openings in order to replace workers who leave these occupations. People who work in educa-tional programs that prepare these workers say that new graduates are still having some trouble finding jobs they desire, but the situa-tion has improved somewhat over the past few years; entry-level jobs in residence hall administration have been especially numer-ous compared to the number of applicants for these positions.

SALARY, OTHER BENEFITS, AND WORKING CONDITIONS

Salary information for many of these jobs is collected by the National Association of Student Personnel Administrators. The following figures come from its 1995–1996 salary survey and covers large colleges and universities.

Position Title	Mean Salary
Senior student affairs officer	79,744
Registrar	51,348
Director, student financial aid	50,746
Director, student union	44,833
Director, counseling services	49,731
Admissions director	55,488
Director, student housing	44,951
Placement director	43,933

As always, the mean or median salaries listed fail to show the considerable variation found in each occupation. Those who work at smaller institutions might earn considerably less. For example, the salaries of most career counselors in 1996 ranged from about $26,500 per year to $46,200. In 1996, the median salary for all full-time vocational counselors was $36,100. The size of the school and whether it is privately run or publicly supported generally affects salaries a good deal—but not always.

Student affairs workers enjoy the usual fringe benefits of college and university employees, including health insurance and pension programs. In many cases, they also pay reduced tuition rates and have the use of school recreational facilities. The cost of attending workshops, meetings, or conventions is also paid by the school in many cases. The physical working conditions are usually pleasant.

ENTRY REQUIREMENTS AND CAREER LADDER

Educational requirements vary somewhat from position to position. In general, a master's degree in student personnel and an internship served in a postsecondary institution is the minimum required; applicants with doctorates are preferred. According to a National Association of Student Personnel Administrators' survey of several years ago, more than 60 percent of chief student affairs officers and officers for counseling held doctorates; by contrast, the highest degree for the officer for student financial aid was a bachelor's degree in 23 percent of the cases. Positions at smaller schools are frequently held by graduates of the institution. Furthermore, surveys of people in student affairs often turn up a variety of educational backgrounds. For example, while the most common academic specialty for career planning and placement directors surveyed by the College Placement Council was guidance and counseling, directors also had degrees in education, business administration, student personnel, higher education administration, education administration, counseling psychology, English, and psychology.

Among the titles for graduate programs that prepare these workers besides student personnel are college student development, student personnel services, community college counseling, community college management, community college leadership, student development in higher education, counseling and student personnel, college student personnel administration, and pupil and student personnel services. These programs are usually housed in a department of counselor education in a school of education. Between seventy to ninety programs are available nationwide.

People hired for counseling positions often need a doctorate in counseling, counseling psychology, or clinical psychology. One survey of campus counseling centers found that 65 percent of the directors had doctorates. About half the professionals on their staffs were licensed; these were evenly divided between psychologists and counselors.

The direction most people's careers will take becomes apparent while they are graduate students. Typically they will begin to focus on a specialty, such as financial aid or placement, and serve their practicum or internship in that field. A person's experience before earning a graduate degree may also affect his or her career; for example, nonacademic work experience is an invaluable asset to career counselors, according to the College Placement Council. Transfers from one specialty to another are made by people at various stages of their career, however. Note that teaching experience is not usually needed either for initial employment or advancement, although many people in student affairs do teach.

Advancement in these occupations can occur by moving up the administrative ladder within an institution or by moving from smaller to larger institutions. A doctorate may be required for advancement. The lack of growth projected for postsecondary institutions in general indicates that in the future promotions may be even more difficult to obtain than entry-level jobs.

For more information about these occupations, speak to the people on campus who have them. Information is also available in the books and journals listed in Appendix B. Among the associations whose members work in one of these occupations are the College Placement Council, National Association of Student Activity Advisers, National Association of Student Financial Aid Administrators, National Association of Student Personnel Administrators, the American College Counselors Association, and the American College Personnel Association of the American Counseling Association; addresses and more information for each are given in Appendix A. Jobs in these fields are advertised in the newsletters and journals of the associations and in the *Chronicle for Higher Education.*

CHAPTER 11

EMPLOYMENT AND CAREER COUNSELORS: FACTS AND FIGURES

OTHER JOB TITLES

Vocational counselor, career development specialist, job counselor. Career management professional.

GOALS AND DUTIES

Employment and career counselors assist clients in choosing and preparing for a career and in finding a suitable job. Career management professional is a popular title in the private sector firms; employment counselor is a title that's often associated with government service.

The basic duties of an employment counselor are interviewing, testing, counseling, referral to other agencies, and placement. Clients can come from any age group or employment background, and the counselor's duties naturally vary somewhat depending on the client's needs. The services that will benefit a young, single, recently discharged veteran may be of little use to a middle-aged steel worker who has a family and a mortgage. State agencies provide specialized services for groups such as veterans, youth, women, recipients of Aid for Dependent Children, older workers, the disabled, rural residents, and the economically disadvantaged.

An employment counselor usually begins by interviewing the client in order to learn what skills, experience, and education the client can bring to an employer. The counselor may then determine that additional aptitude and interest tests are needed. The counselor reviews the results of these tests with the client and assists the client in identifying suitable occupations. The counselor may find that the client needs further education or training and then provide information on suitable programs and financial aid. Or the client may simply need help with job-seeking skills that can be developed in group sessions. The counselor may act as a leader for such a group or job club. In other cases, the client may need no more than a job referral or assistance with a résumé. No matter where the client starts in relation to the world of work, the ultimate goal of client and counselor is placement in a specific job. Counselors then conduct follow-up interviews with former clients and their employers in order to learn the success of the placement.

Besides working on the clearly vocational concerns described above, these counselors also seek to reduce the psychological impact of unemployment and help people survive while unemployed. This might entail referring clients to other agencies or individual and group counseling sessions on subjects such as stress management and living on a reduced income.

Employment counseling requires knowledge of the work world as well as interviewing and counseling skills. The success of the counselor's office or agency depends in part on the counselor's relations with employers. The future will see more career centers for adults and more online job databases, in the continuing effort to match jobs to talent.

EMPLOYMENT AND OUTLOOK

There are currently several thousand employment counselors. Of these, about 50 percent are with state agencies and the rest with private companies or other agencies. However, precise employment figures for state agencies, once collected by the federal government, are no longer available, and the total given is at best an educated guess. In 1996, roughly eight hundred career counselors were certified as National Certified Career Counselors by the National Board for Certified Counselors.

Most employment counselors work for agencies of the state government that are largely supported by federal funds. The agency is usually called the Job Service, but other titles include the Employment Service and the Employment Security Agency. Counselors with the Job Service may either counsel full time or spend half their time or more in such noncounseling activities as intake interviewing, taking orders for job banks, administering tests, certifying program applicants, or leading job-search workshops.

Most private employment agencies employ few if any of these types of counselors because they are primarily concerned with rapidly placing individuals in jobs for which they have proven experience and not with career exploration. Besides the Job Service, therefore, the most likely employers are community agencies. In some cases, counselors in private practice specialize in employment concerns. A small but growing source of jobs has been the movement by large corporations to provide outplacement counseling to fired workers, especially at the executive level. The counselor may work directly for the corporation or, more often, for a private firm that contracts with the large company to provide the outplacement services.

The employment of counselors in state agencies declined slowly throughout the 1970s and then plummeted in the early 1980s as approximately one-third of the positions with the Job Service were cut. Nationwide, employment is declining, often through attrition.

This trend is not expected to change. But funding decisions, which were once made by Congress, are now determined locally. In 1996, welfare reform legislation passed, with the effect of giving states more power over their welfare programs. The situation varies dramatically from state to state and even from city to city. It also changes every year, along with political conditions.

Employment is growing in the private sector, although employment lags behind the need for these services. The number of new positions will probably be relatively small in terms of the economy as a whole. One possible source of employment growth in the private sector is with firms that, under contract, provide services similar to those once provided by the government's Job Service.

Another possible source of employment is as a career development specialist with a corporation or large government agency. United Auto Workers' contracts with the Ford Motor Company, for example, and sometimes sets aside money to pay for the career counseling of laid-off workers; a single development such as this can lead to an increase in the number of counselors in private practice who have duties similar to those of an employment counselor.

The potential for private sector employment for counselors in career development is subject to dispute within the business community. At least one corporation hires only counseling psychologists with a doctorate for its program. Another one expresses reluctance to consider hiring people with any graduate degree from counselor education programs—the term *counselor* is viewed negatively. Businesses generally prefer to hire people with a degree in human relations development, in part because businesses are concerned that people trained in counselor education programs would be more interested in counseling individuals than in program management, which would be their primary duty. Whatever the reasons, career development programs in corporations are frequently administered by individuals who entered the corporate world after receiving undergraduate degrees and working in the corporation's human resources department.

Counselors are being hired by corporations and agencies, however, especially if they can show an understanding of business as demonstrated in undergraduate course work or familiarity with business gained through an internship dealing with corporate issues and served in a corporate setting. These positions are most appealing to those with an entrepreneurial spirit since the counselor must constantly sell the organization on the value of the service.

SALARY, OTHER BENEFITS, AND WORKING CONDITIONS

Salaries vary a great deal, according to employers. Entry-level earnings generally range from $19,000 to $29,000, with experienced counselors earning over $34,000 per year. A full-time counselor can charge $85 an hour or $400–$1,200 for three to five sessions. The counselor can usually log 20 to 30 contact hours a week.

Employment counselors who work for the state enjoy the usual benefits of state employees. Those who work for the private sector also receive benefits, although the benefits package might not be as generous.

ENTRY REQUIREMENTS AND CAREER LADDER

With fifty state agencies doing much of the hiring, there are fifty sets of entry requirements. In general, states seek people with a bachelor's degree in one of the behavioral sciences or with additional courses in counseling; relevant professional experience can usually be substituted for education. Usually, a person must pass an examination given by the state's civil service or merit hiring board. Many states hire college graduates as employment interviewers; counselors are then trained and chosen from among the interviewers already employed. In other cases, states hire counselor trainees to begin with. To be considered for a promotion, a trainee or an interviewer may need to attend a graduate school program or an agency training program for counselors. A master's in counseling is now preferred. Other programs you can choose to advance your career include career facilitator (less than a master's, but at least 120 hours of classroom training) and—at the upper end of the educational scale, some choose to pursue an M.B.A. in Human Resources with a career development specialization.

Only a few counselor education programs have the kind of emphasis sought by private industry for career development specialists. According to someone associated with these programs, however, the challenge facing graduates is less in proving their qualifications than in uncovering the jobs, because no central clearinghouse advertises these positions. In fact, almost all graduates of counselor education programs do find positions in the private sector or with large government agencies, although these positions are relatively few in number.

Welfare reform, passed in 1996, is bound to make changes in the field, but it will also lead to opportunities, as the government programs mandate a "workfare" program plan. Employment counselors can advance to administrative positions within their agencies.

More information about this occupation is available from the counselor at local Job Service offices; one should be listed in the "state-government" section of your telephone book. General information about employment with state and local governments—including salaries, fringe benefits, and hiring practices—is available in *Opportunities in State and Local Government Careers* by Neale Baxter (Lincolnwood, Ill.: VGM Career Horizons, 1993). The National Board for Certified Counselors (3 Suite D Terrace Way Greensboro, NC 27403) offers certification in a career counseling specialty.

CHAPTER 12

OTHER COUNSELING AND COUNSELING-RELATED OCCUPATIONS

The duties of workers in many occupations are closely related to those of counselors. Indeed, in some cases, drawing a line between counseling and other occupations can be extremely difficult. Among these occupations are alcohol and substance abuse counselors, counseling psychologists, school psychologists, and psychiatrists. Social workers and members of the clergy also use counseling techniques. Counselor educators are professors in graduate school departments that train counselors. Many professionals in the human resources development departments of large corporations also perform duties similar to those of counselors, although they tend to have more administrative responsibilities.

ALCOHOL AND DRUG ABUSE COUNSELOR

People who recognize, or are forced to face, their dependency on alcohol or other drugs often enter programs that provide medical monitoring, structure, an introduction to Alcoholics Anonymous or a similar fellowship, and counseling. The counseling may be conducted by specialists in the field who are known by various titles, such as addiction counselor, alcoholism counselor, chemical dependency counselor, drug abuse counselor, and substance abuse counselor. The counselor's duties include evaluating the client's condition, conducting individual and group counseling sessions, and meeting with other staff members to develop an individualized treatment program for each client. Work settings include hospitals, treatment centers, government agencies, and private practice.

These counselors number more than 25,000 according to the National Association of Alcoholism and Drug Abuse Counselors. The need for such counselors is great, judging by the number of alcoholics (more than twenty million) and other chemically dependent people in the country; but relatively few people seek treatment. Demand is also held down by lack of funds; funding for treatment programs is harder to come by than denunciations of drugs and drunk drivers.

One distinguishing characteristic of this occupation, as opposed to other counseling occupations, is the variety of routes to employment. Although most alcohol and substance abuse counselors have a bachelor's degree, employers may not require one, in part because suitable courses were rarely offered by colleges in the past. This situation has changed, and many two-year and four-year colleges and graduate schools now provide appropriate training. In the absence of a fixed educational requirement, employers seek to hire individuals who have a competency-based certification. Certification requires experience, which can be acquired as a counselor-in-training. Employers hiring counselors-in-training look for people who have good counseling skills and are knowledgeable about the substances being abused, the nature of alcoholism and addiction, and the resources available to a recovering individual.

Certification of these counselors is available through states and other jurisdictions; it is often voluntary, but in all states there is some form of recognition or certification, either through state government or privately. No single national certification board exists; however, the National Commission on Accreditation of Alcoholism and Drug Abuse Credentialing Bodies has set standards for the states to follow. The minimum standards for certification usually include at least two years of supervised work experience as an alcoholism or drug abuse counselor, two hundred to three hundred clock hours of training, a written test, and a case presentation. Dual certification for alcohol and other drugs requires three years of supervised experience and is becoming increasingly important. More than thirty credentialing bodies have accepted these standards. The top level of certification is represented by Master Addictions Counselor, which requires a master's degree, 500 contact hours of training, and a passing grade on the MAC exam administered by the National Board of Certified Counselors. Three years of experience are also required, two of which must be post-master's degree.

No national salary data have been collected, but these counselors earn approximately $19,000 to $29,000 a year; these earnings are generally less than those of nurses or social workers. Counselors in publicly funded programs perceive themselves as low paid.

More information about these workers appears in "Treating Addictions" by Michael Stanton in the *Occupational Outlook Quarterly,* Winter 1988. You can learn the names of local counselors to talk to about the occupation by contacting one of the programs listed under "alcoholism" in the yellow pages. *Directory of Academic Institutions and Organizations: Drug, Alcohol, and Employment Assistant Program Educational Resources* is a comprehensive listing of training programs published by the National Institute on Drug Abuse, U.S. Department of Health and Human Services. Single copies of the bulletin are available free while the supply lasts from the National Clearinghouse for Alcohol and Drug Information, P.O. Box 2345, Rockville, Maryland 20852, (301) 468-2600.

COUNSELING PSYCHOLOGIST

According to the American Psychological Association (APA), counseling psychologists "provide services to promote individual and group well-being and to prevent and remedy developmental, educational, vocational, social and/or emotional adjustment problems." Like other counselors, they usually work with clients considered normal rather than patients considered ill; they are qualified to work with the maladjusted, however.

Although precise figures are unavailable, employment probably exceeds six thousand; almost three thousand members of the APA state that they are employed full time as counseling psychologists. Only clinical psychology is more often identified as a specialty by APA members; clinical psychology, however, is mentioned almost four times as often. The major employment settings for counseling psychologists who belong to Division 17 of the APA are schools, counseling centers, and private practice. More than 40 percent have private practice as their secondary employment setting, while it is the primary setting for 15 percent; the growing importance of private practice is indicated by the finding that younger counseling psychologists are twice as likely as older ones to be engaged in private practice. Other employment settings are hospitals, community mental health centers, full-time consultation, and government agencies.

In recent years, between 300 and 450 doctorates a year were awarded in counseling psychology. Surveys of previous classes found fewer than ten of the new doctors being unemployed, indicating that the supply does not currently exceed the demand. Even a very slow rate of growth, coupled with normal turnover, would suffice to make employment opportunities for new graduates favorable in this occupation.

The average salary of licensed psychologists with a doctorate who provided direct human services was more than $50,000 in

1991; those with a master's degree earned $38,000, on average. Counseling psychologists enjoy the usual fringe benefits granted by their employer.

Fully qualified counseling psychologists have a doctorate in their field from a program accredited by the APA. Use of the job title *psychologist* by people who are offering services to the public is controlled in every state. Common requirements, besides the doctorate, are one to two years of experience and successful performance on an examination. A list of these boards and their addresses is available from the APA, whose address is in Appendix A.

More information about this occupation is available in *Opportunities in Psychology Careers* by Donald E. Super and Charles M. Super (Lincolnwood, Ill.: VGM Career Horizons, 1988) and in the other sources of information listed in the appendixes.

COUNSELOR EDUCATOR

Counselor educators instruct and train future counselors, usually in graduate school counselor education programs. Their duties and the degree of their specialization vary greatly, depending on the size and emphasis of the program with which they are associated. As university professors, they are responsible for designing courses, lecturing, assigning research projects, and evaluating the progress of students. Many conduct original research. They also supervise prospective counselors during practicums and internships. Counselor educators like Dr. Scalise, who is interviewed in an earlier chapter, often combine their professorial duties with a counseling practice, either in association with the school's counseling center or in private.

According to Joseph Hollis and Richard Wantz, there are about twice as many part-time counselor educators as full-time. Universities are the major employers. A counselor education program may have a single full-time faculty member and a couple of part-time teachers; large programs employ twenty or more instructors and professors.

The general outlook for college professors is poor because of the projected decline in the number of eighteen- to twenty-five-year-olds, the group that traditionally has accounted for the majority of college students. This trend projection should be viewed with caution for two reasons. First, it is not necessarily relevant to the outlook for any particular teaching specialty. Because of the many different specialties of college teachers and the relatively small number of people in each, no particular outlook information is usually available. In the case of counselor educators, employment will rise if a favorable job market for counselors begins to attract large numbers of students to the field. Second, high school students considering this occupation will not be prepared to enter it until after the year 2000, by which time the number of eighteen-year-olds will have risen.

A Ph.D. in counseling or a related field is generally required for these positions. Among the specialties within the field are school, rehabilitation, and marriage and family therapy. Almost 90 percent of all counselor educators do in fact have doctorates. Those with only a master's degree are most likely to be part-time instructors or graduate students completing their doctoral programs.

The average nine- or ten-month salary in student counseling and personnel services ranged from about $22,602 for instructors to $40,472 for full professors in public senior colleges and universities and college and university teachers, according to one survey in the early 1990s. Besides the usual fringe benefits, professors may be granted sabbaticals by their schools in order to pursue research projects.

College teachers usually begin their careers as either instructors or assistant professors, later advancing to the ranks of associate and full professor. Advancement often hinges on publication or other evidence of a growing reputation in a person's field.

The American Association of University Professors, 1012 14th Street, Suite 500, Washington, D.C. 20005, can provide information about college and university teaching in general. The Association for Counselor Education and Supervision represents counselor educators within the American Counseling Association, 5999 Stevenson Avenue, Alexandria, Virginia 22304. Faculty members of counselor education programs—especially the largest ones—are the best sources of information about the nature of the work and the current and projected job market in this field.

MEMBER OF THE CLERGY

Many members of the clergy—ministers, priests, and rabbis—devote much of their time to counseling activities. More than three thousand are members of the American Association of Pastoral Counselors, 9508A Lee Highway, Fairfax, Virginia 22031. Although counseling may become the primary duty of many clerics, they usually follow this vocation for other reasons. The decision to enter the clergy should be based on one's religious convictions. *Opportunities in Religious Service Careers,* by John Oliver Nelson (Lincolnwood, Ill.: VGM Career Horizons, 1988), discusses why a person should enter the clergy and offers practical advice to those interested in a religion-oriented career.

Some counselor education programs in universities have programs in pastoral counseling. Members of the clergy who wish to receive training in counseling can also contact the Association for Clinical Pastoral Education, Inc., 1549 Clairmont Road, Suite 103, Decatur, Georgia 30033, (404) 320-1472. It accredits and publishes a directory of supervisors and training centers in hospitals, other health care institutions, and prisons.

PARAPROFESSIONAL

The term *paraprofessional* usually refers to a job that does not require a college degree. Medicine now employs many paraprofessionals in a variety of technical occupations. No comparable growth has occurred in counseling, where the term is used loosely of workers who take over some of the noncounseling functions in an office, such as updating a referral directory. Paraprofessionals in counseling are likely to have entered the field as clerical workers and then taken on more responsibility as they gained experience.

Rehabilitation has seen some growth in employment of people with less than a counselor's training. These individuals are usually college graduates, however, often having attended an undergraduate program in rehabilitation services. Although they may be referred to as paraprofessionals, they would be classified as professionals by most of the organizations that collect employment data.

PSYCHIATRIST

Psychiatrists are medical doctors who diagnose and treat mental illnesses. Although they may use counseling or psychological techniques, they may also prescribe drugs or electroshock therapy. They are the only mental health professionals authorized to prescribe drugs.

Psychiatrists may have a general practice or they may specialize in a field such as industrial psychiatry, forensic psychiatry, or psychoanalysis. Child psychiatry is considered a separate specialty by the American Medical Association.

Of all the medical doctors in America, about 10 percent are psychiatrists, according to the American Medical Association. About half have full-time private practices. Administrating community mental health centers, teaching in medical school, and conducting research are among the duties of other psychiatrists, often in combination with a part-time private practice.

The average net earnings for psychiatrists was more than $90,000 in 1990, according to the American Medical Association. Although these earnings are much higher than those in other occupations, they are lower than the average net earnings of all physicians, which exceed $106,300 a year.

Psychiatrists must be licensed to practice medicine, which means that they must graduate from an accredited medical school and pass the appropriate examinations. Entrance into medical school is extremely competitive. Generally, psychiatrists spend four years in residency programs after medical school and then take exams administered by the American Board of Psychiatry and Neurology.

Physicians have enjoyed a very favorable job market for the past generation, at least in part because of the restrictions on the number of students in medical schools. In the future, physicians starting a practice are expected to face somewhat more competition than they have recently. Psychiatry, which is entered by so few medical school graduates, should be less competitive.

More information about this occupation is available from the Office of Related Health Professions, American Medical Association, 515 North State Street, Chicago, Illinois 60610, (312) 464-5000. The Association of American Medical Colleges, One Dupont Circle, N.W., Washington, D.C. 20036, (202) 828-0400, can provide a list of approved medical schools and general information on premedical education, financial aid, and medicine as a profession.

PUPIL PERSONNEL WORKER

These professionals visit the homes of students who have not been attending school. They speak to the child's parents or guardians, seeking to learn the reason for the student's absence. Reasons can include fear of school, a lack of proper clothing or nutrition, or other problems. The pupil personnel worker seeks a solution, which can require referral to other agencies, such as the social services department. Counseling during the course of several visits may be necessary before the problem is resolved. If there are pockets of truancy within a building or neighborhood, the pupil personnel worker may contact other agencies of the government, such as the recreation department, to set up tutorial or other educational programs outside the school. Other job titles for these workers are attendance workers, truant officers, and visiting teachers.

Employment figures for this occupation are not collected. Employment could easily exceed ten thousand, however, since one worker would be needed for every two thousand to four thousand students. Detailed salary information is not available either. Salaries for these workers are certainly somewhat higher than those of teachers, however, and are often supplemented by a travel allowance. Employment is usually year-round.

These are not entry-level positions. The typical pupil personnel worker has several years experience within a school system as a teacher, administrator, or counselor in addition to specialized training, such as a master's degree in guidance. Recruitment is usually conducted within the school system. All states certify these workers. Although there is an International Association of Pupil Personnel Workers, the best sources of additional information about this occupation are the state departments of education —listed in Appendix C—and local school districts.

SCHOOL PSYCHOLOGIST

School psychologists, like school counselors, work to improve the intellectual, social, and emotional development of children.

According to the National Association of School Psychologists, Inc., school psychology "focuses upon the psycho-educational development of individuals, their abilities and potentialities, and the emotional and cultural factors which influence this learning process."

As with other occupations, their duties vary with the employer. In some school districts they practically function as elementary school counselors, providing counseling and consultation services to the students and teachers in two or three schools. In others, school psychologists might work almost exclusively as counselors for students with adjustment problems or with families undergoing unusual stress. In yet another, school psychologists will be actively engaged in curriculum development or in-service training.

School psychologists, being responsible for the placement of students in programs that will be most beneficial, often have a special concern with assessment. Assessment is based on a psycho-educational evaluation of the student's personal social adjustment, intelligence, academic achievement, sensory and perceptual motor functioning, and environmental or cultural influences. On average, school psychologists spend 40 percent of their time on assessment and the rest on intervention, which includes counseling and other duties.

Total employment exceeds twenty thousand. Federal law mandates that states allocate funds for the employment of one school psychologist for every two thousand students. Current employment approaches that goal, according to several studies. Little growth is expected. However, even slight growth coupled with normal turnover will result in numerous openings per year. Shortages exist in medium-size cities as well as in large urban and small rural districts. The recognition of this situation by one school board caused it to use Federal Express to send its job announcements to graduate schools. In other words, the job market is good now and expected to get even better.

Comprehensive salary data is not collected for this occupation. A survey of its members by the National Association of School Psychologists found that 50 percent of the respondents were earning between $22,000 and $34,000 a year; salaries lower than $13,000 and higher than $52,000 were also reported. In 1996 the latest data showed a $45,000 median salary for school psychologists with a doctorate, according to the U.S. Department of Labor.

A fully qualified school psychologist has a master's degree plus about seventy-two graduate school credits in school psychology as well as supervised experience in the field. Such an education program leads to an educational specialist degree, which requires roughly twice the number of credits that a master's degree does. Doctorate programs are also available. In recent years, the number of students proceeding to a doctorate has increased, in part because of the status of the doctorate as the entry-level degree for other psychology specialties. Master's and doctorate programs are accredited by the National Council for the Accreditation of Teacher Education, 2010 Massachusetts, N.W., Suite 500, Washington, D.C. 20036–1023, (202) 466-7496. It publishes a list of programs annually. School psychologists must be certified by their state's department of education or department of public instruction (addresses are listed in Appendix C). Certification as a school psychologist is not a license to practice psychology.

More information about this occupation is available from the National Association of School Psychologists, Inc., 4340 East West Highway, Suite 402, Bethesda, Maryland, 20814–4411, (301) 657–0270. It currently has about fifteen thousand members. Information also appears in *Opportunities in Psychology Careers* by Donald E. Super and Charles M. Super (Lincolnwood, Ill.:

VGM Career Horizons, 1988) and the other sources of information listed in the appendixes.

SOCIAL WORKER

Social workers—who are much more numerous than counselors —provide counseling for individuals, families, and groups. Among their other duties are the administration of aid programs and the referral of clients to other agencies for some services, such as job training or day care. The speedy identification of a client's needs and the implementation of a plan to supply essential food, shelter, clothing, and medical attention probably account for more of the average social worker's time than does counseling. Individual social workers, however, may be primarily concerned with counseling.

Social workers may specialize in particular fields. About half of all social workers are in just three categories: mental health, child/ youth, and medical/health. Those working in mental health frequently work in a community mental health clinic or outpatient psychiatric clinic, helping patients adjust to their conditions. Child welfare workers counsel children; advise and consult with parents, teachers, and others; arrange for homemaker services; and start legal action to protect neglected or abused children. Medical social workers help patients and their families plan for discharges and work to coordinate the services of the many different agencies that provide help to people in need.

Social workers usually have an eight-hour day, five days a week. Part of their time is spent in comfortable offices, but they must also visit clients.

The usual educational requirement is a bachelor's degree in social work, psychology, or sociology. A bachelor's degree in social work includes courses in human behavior, social work methods, social welfare policies, and supervised field experience. Some positions require a master of social work degree.

More than forty states require that social workers be licensed or registered.

Salaries for social workers ranged from $20,000 to $45,000 a year in 1994. They vary widely by setting, experience, and duties. Social workers receive the usual fringe benefits.

More than 557,000 people worked as social workers in 1994. The major employers are departments of human resources, social services, mental health, housing, education, and correction. Many private organizations also provide social services and employ social workers, including community service organizations, religious communities, and large corporations. Furthermore, social workers, like counselors, are increasingly entering private practice.

The number of social workers is rising faster than the average for all occupations. Many positions will become available because of turnover, which is relatively high for this occupation. The needs of a growing and aging population will also increase the demand for workers in this field.

More information about this occupation is available from the following associations.

National Association of Social Workers
750 First Street, N.E., Suite 700
Washington, DC 20002–4241

Council on Social Work Education
1600 Duke Street
Alexandria, VA 22314
(703) 683-8080

Information also appears in *Opportunities in Social Work Careers* by Renee Wittenberg (Lincolnwood, Ill.: VGM Career Horizons, 1996). General information about employment with state and local governments—including salaries, fringe benefits, and hiring practices—is available in *Opportunities in State and Local Government Careers* by Neale Baxter (Lincolnwood, Ill.: VGM Career Horizons, 1993) and in *Careers in Social and Rehabilitation Services,* by Geraldine Garner (Lincolnwood, Ill: VGM Career Horizons, 1994).

CHAPTER 13

CHARACTERISTICS OF A COUNSELOR

Can I see another's woe / And not be in sorrow too?
Can I see another's grief / And not seek for kind relief?

—William Blake

WHAT MAKES A GOOD COUNSELOR?

When describing the characteristics of counselors, some writers sound almost as though they are talking about Claire and Cliff Huxtable, the parents on "The Cosby Show." The combination of concern for individuals, empathy, emotional stability, patience, objectivity, and sense of humor that they demonstrate is mentioned again and again.

Empathy usually leads the list. By empathy, writers mean more than sympathy. They mean that the counselor doesn't just feel sorry for the client but can actually identify with the client, can take a hike in the client's Reeboks. Empathy implies other important characteristics. For example, a counselor must be broadminded, sensitive to others, tolerant, and understanding, recognizing people's right to be different. Without these qualities, counselors cannot work effectively with a range of clients. C. Gilbert Wrenn, the respected author of *The World of the Contemporary Counselor,* alludes to these important qualities when he writes, "I have begun to think that the ability to listen with understanding, and without apparent threat to either counselor or client, is a most important attribute of an effective counselor."

Empathy is not enough, of course. Counseling is an alternating current. Not only must a counselor identify with a client, the client must recognize the counselor's concern. Successful counselors are friendly, pleasant, and tactful. They like people—seeing others as able, dependable, and worthy—and people like counselors. They are sincere, and people recognize their sincerity. They are trustworthy, and people see them as such.

Counselors cannot wallow in a sea of emotion, however, or confuse the client's success with their own. Although empathy is essential in both identifying the client's problems and winning the client's trust, objectivity is needed to find solutions. Solutions also require a thorough knowledge of possibilities and respect for facts. Typical counselors, therefore, would score well on both the verbal and mathematical components of aptitude tests. They are alert and can communicate clearly with all sorts of people.

Besides understanding others, counselors must understand themselves. They must recognize their own strengths and accept their own weaknesses. Their sense of humor goes hand in hand with self-knowledge, for it helps keep them levelheaded and tolerant of ambiguity. It goes without saying that their sense of humor is directed at themselves and not—ever—at a client.

The preceding paragraphs describe a counselor's characteristics. A slightly different way to show what an occupation requires is to discuss the skills needed. If the primary characteristic of counselors is empathy, their primary skill is interviewing. It is interviewing skills that enable them to move from testing and providing information to counseling individuals or leading groups.

DOWNERS AND UPPERS

Every silver lining has a cloud, and every occupation has its drawbacks. Satisfaction for a worker occurs only when the positive features of the profession outweigh the downside. Counseling has its share of negative attributes.

Counselors are subject to adverse criticism, some of it contradictory. One group will claim that counseling is an inefficient waste of money while another complains that counselors spend too much time playing games with "interesting" problems and not enough on the average client. A counselor who works for a program supported by tax money—as most do—is especially vulnerable to attacks of inefficiency, because the attack can affect both self-esteem and funding, resulting in poorer performance.

Besides general criticism, counselors are also subject to second guessing by parents, other relatives, and friends of the client. No matter how unfounded, such criticism is not likely to be pleasant. In order to be satisfied with this occupation, a person must be able to shrug off such criticism or—better—to find in it suggestions for improvement.

Yet another downer is that no counselor can be successful with every client. Students turn away from their future, people remain unemployed, alcoholics relapse, and families break apart despite the best effort of the counselor. Accepting such failures is probably a counselor's most difficult task.

Less pressing negative aspects of the occupation have already been alluded to. Counseling is not a way to great wealth or prestige. These are minor complaints for most practicing counselors, who, typically, are more concerned about administrative pressures and a lack of time to counsel than they are about their salary.

What does the satisfied counselor balance against these downers? The client's success. Counselors who enjoy their work like working closely with others and showing them how to achieve their goals. Simply engaging in this kind of activity is rewarding to them. The greatest reward, however, is when the client uses the tools provided by the counselor to actually reach the set goal. Not that the counselor can take credit for the client's work, of course. Just as a good Little League coach never claims victory when the team wins, counselors do not confuse their efforts with the client's. Still, counselors feel great satisfaction when a course of action they have taken with a client pays off in greater success for that client.

No one has all the attributes of a successful, satisfied counselor in full measure. You will probably be most satisfied as a counselor, however, if you have a deep desire to help others along with the willingness and ability to do the hard work required to learn how to help.

CHAPTER 14

EDUCATION FOR COUNSELORS

There are some things which cannot be learned quickly, and time, which is all we have, must be paid heavily for their acquiring.

—Ernest Hemingway

Effective counseling in our complicated world requires more than the personality characteristics described in the last chapter. It also requires a solid academic background. Most positions for counselors require at least a master's degree; earning one usually takes at least one year of full-time study after college. Accredited Ph.D. programs require at least three years of full-time study and an additional year of supervised experience. Students must begin their educational planning in high school to make sure that they will qualify for college.

In college, prospective counselors have four possible options; they might, however, be restricted to a single academic major, depending on their state's regulations governing certification in the specialty they plan to enter. If the student's only concern is admission to graduate school, any academic major will do in most cases since counselor education programs in graduate schools usually accept students without regard to major, although many programs require applicants to have three to five undergraduate courses in psychology or another behavioral science. A second option—the one usually recommended—is to major in psychology or another behavioral science. A third possibility for undergraduates is to major in counselor education. About seventy colleges and universities have such a program, and about thirty offer a bachelor's degree in rehabilitation services administration. This option may be especially attractive to people planning to enter rehabilitation counseling. An undergraduate major in rehabilitation services can shorten a person's stay in graduate school by a semester or more. Fourth, a student may need to major in education in order to qualify for a teaching position so that he or she can gain required teaching experience.

Students should try to clarify their goals no later than their sophomore year in college. They must first determine the kind of counseling they wish to do. Entry positions in rehabilitation counseling, for example, are more likely to be available to qualified college graduates than positions as school counselors.

The chapters on facts and figures in this book present the usual entry requirements for various specialties. Students should, however, learn precise requirements from credentialing authorities. In particular, students may wish to learn if teaching experience is required of school counselors and if other states recognize the certificate for the student's specialty. The credentialing authorities are listed in Appendix C.

Similarly, general employment requirements are given in this book, but students would do well to learn exact requirements of the employers they are most likely to work for. For example, does your state hire entry-level rehabilitation counselors with a bachelor's degree and no experience? Iowa does not. A state may not require that school counselors have teaching experience, but a local school district might. Also remember that no matter what education is required for entry, additional education may be required for advancement.

Graduate schools can provide information on entry requirements for their programs. Should a school call for certain undergraduate courses, for example, you'll be able to take them before graduation. Entry requirements vary widely by program. On average, master's programs require scores on the Graduate Record Exam (GRE), of at least 459 on the verbal and 455 on the quantitative section. Alternatively, a minimum score of 40 on the Miller Analogy Test may be required. From three to five courses in psychology or counseling are also required by many programs. Other typical requirements are a 2.7 undergraduate grade point average (based on straight A's equaling 4.0), letters of recommendation, personal interviews, and relevant work experience. Requirements for doctoral programs are somewhat higher than those for master's programs.

PICKING A PROGRAM

Almost five hundred institutions offer more than one thousand different programs to prepare counselors. Most programs—even those in counseling psychology, rehabilitation counseling, or mental health counseling—are housed in a school of education; programs are also housed in schools of arts and sciences, however. Programs for different kinds of counselors may be in different departments within a school or institution.

The educational choice, in other words, is wide. You will want to consider many different factors before selecting the schools you wish to apply to. The following are some points to bear in mind:

- Accreditation
- Client emphasis
- Philosophical orientation
- Counseling specialties offered
- Nature and extent of field experience
- Degree requirements

- Correlation of degree requirements with certification requirements
- Degree granted
- Entry requirements
- Location
- Size
- Faculty-student ratio
- Location of field experience
- Placement of recent graduates
- Cost
- Availability of scholarships and loans

Whether or not a program is accredited may be particularly important. As recently as fifteen years ago, no programs were accredited specifically for counseling. Now, many are. But the situation continues to change rapidly. You should be especially careful in evaluating programs that are not accredited and have no plans to seek accreditation.

Numerous general directories of colleges and graduate schools are available; several are listed in Appendix B.

Counselor Preparation, 1996–1998: Programs, Personnel, Trends, by Joseph W. Hollis and Richard A. Wantz, is the ninth edition of the most complete specialized directory of programs in counselor preparation published. In addition to a discussion of trends in counselor education, the book includes detailed descriptions of hundreds of programs. Each description gives a complete list of the faculty, degree(s) awarded, number of male and female graduates in each program per year, credit hour and practicum hour requirements, accreditation, percentage of students receiving financial aid, setting of experiential components, placement setting of graduates, courses recently added, and a statement by the school on the unique features of the program. New editions appear every three years. The publisher is Taylor and Francis, 1900 Frost Road, Suite 101, Bristol, Pennsylvania, 19007, (800) 222-1166.

The accreditation boards for different types of programs publish lists of accredited programs. National boards include the following.

Council for Accreditation of Counseling and Related Educational
   Programs (CACREP)
   5999 Stevenson Avenue
   Alexandria, VA 22304
   (703) 823-9800

CACREP accredits master's degree programs in four areas: community counseling, mental health counseling, school counseling, and student affairs practice in higher education. It also accredits doctoral programs in counselor education and supervision. In 1996, thirty-four programs were accredited. People in counselor education expect that only graduates of accredited programs will be considered for many job openings once a substantial number of schools has been accredited. Write CACREP for a directory.

American Psychological Association (APA)
   Accreditation for Counseling Psychology Programs
   750 First Street, NE
   Washington, DC 20002
   (202) 336-5500

The APA currently accredits doctoral programs in counseling psychology. A directory of all accredited programs in psychology, called *Graduate Study in Psychology,* is published annually. The Association also publishes lists of programs three times a year in its journal, *American Psychologist.*

Foundation for Rehabilitation Counseling Education and Research
   1835 Rohlwing Road
   Rolling Meadows, IL 60008
   (847) 394-1785

The Foundation includes the Council on Rehabilitation Education (CRE), which accredits graduate programs in rehabilitation counseling.

Commission on Accreditation for Marriage and Family Therapy
　　Education
　1133 15th Street, NW, Suite 300
　Washington, DC 20005
　(202) 452-0109

An arm of the American Association for Marriage and Family Therapy, the Commission accredits diploma, master's, doctoral, and certification programs.

National Council for the Accreditation of Teacher Education
　2029 K Street, NW, Suite 500
　Washington, DC 20006
　(202) 466-7496

This organization accredits schools of education; as a minimum, a counselor education program should be housed in a school of education accredited by this board.

Association for Clinical Pastoral Education, Inc.
　1549 Clairmont Road, Suite 103
　Decatur, GA 30033
　(404) 320-1472

An interfaith organization, the Association accredits training programs for members of the clergy who perform counseling. It publishes a directory of training centers, seminaries, and supervisors.

WHAT DO YOU LEARN?

Almost any counselor education program is likely to include course work on career development theory, the use of educational and vocational information, statistics, research methods, testing and measurement, counseling theory and technique, the organization and administration of services and the employment setting, psychological development and human behavior, group counseling procedures, and professional ethics. Supervised counseling experience is also provided through a laboratory, practicum, or internship. Internships follow a practicum and may last a full school year. They are usually set in schools or community agencies, such as rehabilitation agencies, mental health clinics, hospitals, marriage and family counseling centers, correctional institutions, diagnostic centers, or employment agencies. Employers often consider the appropriateness of the setting of the internship when comparing the merits of different applicants. For example, the likelihood of your being employed in the private sector is very much improved if you have performed an internship in such a setting.

Hollis and Wantz once classified the educational experiences offered in counselor education programs into eight categories, ranging from cognitive (traditional classroom procedures) to conjoint (the sharing of duties with a working professional). From their list, it is evident that all the following methods are used to educate counselors: readings, discussions, lectures, research projects, video recordings, films, observation of counseling sessions, role playing, field trips, internships, and work as a student counselor under supervision.

Differences among the programs for various specialties can appear at any point. For example, a program for secondary school counselors might require a course in adolescent psychology while the elementary school program specifies child psychology. Programs accredited by CACREP must require these core courses: human growth and development, social and cultural foundations, helping relationships, groups, life-style and career development, appraisal, research and evaluation, and professional orientation. CRE-accredited programs require courses on the principles and practice of rehabilitation counseling; medical aspects of disability; and utilizing community resources. The model curriculum proposed by the American Association for Marriage and Family Therapy requires two to four courses in each of the following three areas: marriage and family systems, marriage and family therapy, and individual development. The differences are greatest, however, in the particular internship, practicum, or supervised counseling that the student engages in. These programs are changed and updated regularly.

The average practicum in a master's program lasts two hundred contact hours and the average internship three hundred to six hundred hours; both practicums and internships are twice as long in doctoral programs. The length of these experiences varies according to the student's specialty. Marriage and family therapy programs typically require more supervised experience and school or student affairs programs less. The Ed.D. programs also tend to require less supervised experience than the Ph.D. programs.

WHAT IS IT LIKE?

This chapter gives a rather dry rundown of requirements and course offerings. Counseling is not simply academic, however, and counselor education is not simply the mastery of information. Students in a counselor education program go through the emotions of fear, testing, discovery, and fuller realization of self.

TRENDS TO KEEP TRACK OF

Current issues in counseling are discussed in a subsequent chapter. Some of them are directly related to counselor education, however. In particular, the number of credit hours required in accredited programs is greater than the requirements of traditional master's degree programs in most fields. Roughly thirty-six semester hours are required in most programs, but accredited counselor-preparation programs require forty-eight. The amount of time spent in supervised counseling is also greater than was required in most programs before the accreditation movement got underway. Nevertheless, accredited programs attract more applicants.

Another change affecting education is the increasing specialization of counselors. Not so long ago, almost all programs were designed for school counselors with a few courses on subjects such as marriage and family counseling or rehabilitation counseling offered as electives. Now, however, programs designed specifically for agency counseling, pastoral counseling, and all the other counseling specialties are becoming common. Recently, schools have been adding courses in marriage and family, gerontology, substance abuse, the law, and ethical issues. According to Hollis and Wantz, programs for marriage and family counseling/therapy have been increasing in number while the number of programs for school and rehabilitation counselors has remained stable over the past few years.

CHAPTER 15

COUNSELING'S PAST

The best of prophets of the future is the past.

—George Gordon, Lord Byron

Counseling is an American occupation that grew out of the country's promise to its citizens. The late 1800s, a period of gross materialism and blatant political corruption, is sometimes called the Gilded Age. Gilding is even less than skin deep, however, and underneath the glitter of millionaires, debutantes, and mansions in this period and the following decades was the reality of the muck-rakers and social reformers such as Ida Tarbell and Jacob Riis. Waves of immigrants from Europe and migrants from American farms were flooding the cities. The newcomers looked for hope and opportunity but found disease and destitution. The country was not ready to accept such conditions, however. A series of reform movements providing for settlement houses, improved sanitation, better housing, and access to education helped relieve some of the worst conditions. One of those movements led to the counseling profession that exists today.

EARLY PROGRAMS

Guidance, as counseling was called until recently, had no founder. It is too multifaceted an activity for that. But one person, Frank Parsons, is often called its father; he established the Vocational Bureau in Boston in 1908. Even earlier, George Merril had started a vocational guidance program in San Francisco, and Jessie B. Davis, in Detroit, had devoted classroom time to guidance activities. In 1907, as principal of Central High in Grand Rapids, Michigan, Davis made character development and vocational information part of the curriculum. At this same period, similar programs began in Cincinnati, Chicago, De Kalb (Illinois), Denver, Lincoln (Nebraska), Los Angeles, Minneapolis, New York City, Oakland, Omaha, Providence (Rhode Island), Salt Lake City, and Seattle. Even earlier, books such as *The Book of Trades* or *Library of Useful Arts* had appeared to help people learn about occupations.

The early programs all focused on vocational information, but they were also concerned with discovering how to match individuals with the occupations that would suit them best so that they could fully develop their potential. Parsons, in particular, is credited with making such matching a systematic activity. In *Choosing a Vocation,* he writes that a person must take three steps before selecting a field of work: First, develop a clear understanding of yourself—your aptitudes, abilities, interests, resources, limitations, and other qualities. Second, gain a knowledge of the requirements and conditions of success, advantages and disadvantages, compensations, opportunities, and prospects in different lines of work. Third, achieve true reasoning on the relation of these two groups of facts.

PROGRESS IN COUNSELING

The years that followed saw rapid progress. Counselors organized the National Vocational Guidance Association in 1913. Other organizations followed, many of which merged to form the American Personnel and Guidance Association in 1952. It became the American Association for Counseling and Development in

1984, and it is now known as the American Counseling Association (ACA).

Development of Tests

The work of Sigmund Freud, Carl Jung, and Clifford Beers—who launched the mental hygiene movement—fueled improvements in the treatment of mental illness and initiated programs to identify mental illness early. The development of the intelligence test by Alfred Binet led to great interest in testing and measurement on the part of the army as well as educators. World War I brought about mass testing of individuals for the first time. Improvements in the validity of various tests were made, and even more extensive testing occurred during World War II.

Carl Rogers

Besides testing, the 1940s are important for the publication of *Counseling and Psychotherapy* by Carl Rogers. Rogers stressed the importance of the counseling relationship; his work thus acted as a counterweight to the diagnostic/testing developments of the war. The importance of the clients' or students' own perceptions of their needs was reemphasized.

Government Support

The Great Depression and World War II increased the federal government's support for guidance activity in many ways. This support included funds for research on vocations and training programs for counselors as well as the employment of counselors. The government encouraged counseling in a great many areas; veterans, the unemployed, and elementary schoolchildren were added to those with access to counselors. The National Defense

Education Act of 1958 was especially significant in regard to federal involvement in counseling. One writer, Verne Faust, points to passage of this law as the "beginning of the modern elementary school counseling of any considerable dimension." Its impact is seen in the growing number of school counselors of all types. From 1958 to 1961 their numbers doubled, and the ratio of students to counselors fell dramatically.

The 1960s also saw significant changes in our society's approach to mental health. Successful attempts were made to reduce the number of patients in long-term hospitals. Many factors contributed to this reduction, including the discovery of new drugs that controlled the symptoms of some types of mental illness. Part of the change was also the result of an increased emphasis on comprehensive care, which stressed preventive measures. Counselors played an important part in these programs.

Rehabilitation Services

Rehabilitation became a more important function of counselors after World War II, although earlier efforts had been made. More than 600,000 World War II veterans received rehabilitation services by the end of 1953. Over the years, the number of people eligible for rehabilitation services grew to include the physically disabled, emotionally handicapped, mentally retarded, and recovering substance abusers. The late 1970s saw the inclusion of rehabilitation as a mandatory part of worker's compensation in state laws, beginning with California. The employment of rehabilitation counselors in the private sector has increased significantly as other states have followed suit.

Corporations have also contributed to the growth of the counseling professions. Besides their obvious use of testing and job analysis, they have employed counselors to assist workers with a great many concerns ranging from alcoholism to retirement.

CHAPTER 16

COUNSELING'S PRESENT: APPROACHES AND TECHNIQUES

The ways counselors go about their duties are as varied as the counselors themselves. By and large, however, they make use of certain standard approaches and techniques.

CURRENT APPROACHES TO COUNSELING

In their description of counselor education programs, Joseph Hollis and Richard Wantz identify a dozen different approaches or primary practice orientations that counseling programs might have. An eclectic orientation, in which a counselor does not express a preference for one approach over another, allowing the conditions of the particular case to determine the approach, is the most common. Other common approaches include client centered, behavioral, and cognitive. These four orientations account for about 80 percent of all approaches. Other orientations include existential/humanistic, interpersonal relationship, psychoanalytical, rational/emotive, Gestalt, social learning, systems oriented, and transactional analysis.

Client-centered Counseling

Client-centered or person-centered counseling derives from the work of Carl Rogers. Its importance is understood most easily in light of the situation that prevailed in the 1940s when Rogers first began to publish. At that time, guidance was closely associated with testing. Rogers, whose theories derive in part from the experience of psychotherapists (he was one), stressed that the client, rather than the test, should be at the center of counseling. A client-centered approach sees the warm, trusting relationship between counselor and client as crucial to the success of the counseling. To establish such a relationship, the counselor must accept the client's perception of a situation rather than rely on outside measures, such as tests. In philosophy, the idea that a person's perceptions are the only reality is a basic thesis of phenomenology; thus, this approach is sometimes called phenomenological.

Behavioral Counseling

Behavioral counseling derives from the work of psychologists such as B. F. Skinner. The client decides on the change in behavior sought, but the counselor determines the techniques and procedures to be used. The counselor can even be seen as manipulating the client. Behavioral therapy has been very successful in dealing with some problems, such as stress, in which relief of symptoms is sufficient.

Psychoanalytical Approaches

Psychoanalytical approaches to counseling derive from Sigmund Freud's theories of human nature. According to Freud, people have psychological problems when their ego (or conscious self) fails to balance their id (desire for pleasure) against their superego (the thundering NO! of society).

Existentialism

Existentialism can refer to the somewhat different philosophies of various writers, including Jean Paul Sartre, Albert Camus, Martin Heidegger, and Soren Kierkegaard. In counseling, an existential approach aims at the clients' accepting responsibility for their own actions.

Rational-Emotive Approaches

Rational-emotive or cognitive approaches share with existentialism an emphasis on the individual's responsibility for self-development. Its particular emphasis is that the individual takes control through reason. Among its proponents is Albert Ellis.

Classifications such as those used here always carry the danger that they will be applied too rigidly. In the earlier chapters, you have seen counselors taking various approaches to different problems. In reading over these approaches, you have probably thought of cases in which different theories would be most effective. Indeed, according to Dr. Herr's testimony, researchers have found that, "Regardless of the different theoretical positions that guide the specific techniques used by particular counselors, counselors found to be therapeutic in their interactions with counselees tend to share many common characteristics." An eclectic approach is most often mentioned in every survey. Less important than the philosophical basis of the counselor are the basic principles of guidance—the recognition of the dignity and worth of the individual and the acceptance of the individual's right to choose his or her own future.

INTERVIEWING AND GROUP COUNSELING

Besides a concern with theory, counselor trainees should be aware of the techniques used by counselors. Interviews and group sessions are the tools most often used.

Examples of well-conducted interviews appear frequently in counseling journals and in the books on counseling listed in Appendix B. The principles are easily summarized. Counselors must prepare in advance by reviewing the client's records or consulting with others. The counselor should put the client at ease. The reason for the client's presence should then be established, but the counselor must be aware that the stated reason is not always the real reason. The counselor must let the client take the lead in the interview; this is accomplished by asking open questions and by reflecting what the client says rather than the counselor introducing his or her own ideas. As the interview progresses, the counselor encourages the client to consider the next step to be taken—a test, an action, a review of the problem. The client then may summarize what has been accomplished in the interview. The counselor accompanies the client to the door.

Group counseling has many advantages in certain situations. It enables the counselor to work with more people in less time, establishes peer relationships among the counselees, and sometimes leads them to accept suggestions from each other that they would not entertain from the counselor. Groups work well for individuals who can talk about their concerns, need the reactions of others, and find the support of their peers helpful. They also benefit those who need to develop social skills or get in touch with other people. The determination of who can benefit from group sessions is one of the most difficult for a counselor to make.

CHAPTER 17

CURRENT ISSUES IN COUNSELING

The present is big with the future.

—Leibnitz

One of the things that is not new under the sun is that professions change as society develops new needs. Once we needed horse traders; now we rely on automobile sales representatives. Counseling, too, is subject to changes in society. Some of these changes, such as the growing size of the adult population, are certain. Others, such as the payment of counselors by insurers, are not. These changes have raised important issues for counseling. Other important issues concerning the education that counselors need and the proper role for counselors in society are as old as the occupation. They are not likely to be resolved anytime soon.

THIRD-PARTY PAYMENT

Factors such as the changing age structure of the population and new technology—which may result in more career switching—are fueling possible changes in the rate of growth for particular specialties and increasing the types of settings in which counselors are employed. Demand for services does not necessarily mean that the services will be purchased, however. Not all who want a new car can afford to buy one. The actual growth of counseling, therefore, depends not only on the number of potential clients but also on their willingness and ability to pay for counseling services. It is not possible to gauge the degree of either. However, there would be a greater stimulus to growth if people were able to pay for counseling indirectly—through health insurance, for example. It is for this reason that the question of third-party payment— the payment of the counselor by someone other than the client—is so important.

Third-party payment is somewhat common. Almost 60 percent of the certified clinical mental health counselors responding to a recent survey received third-party payments. In some cases, payment is made through another professional. For example, a counselor may provide services in partnership with a physician. The insurer reimburses the physician who, in turn, pays the counselor.

Counselors are not now reimbursed under Medicare or Medicaid programs, although language authorizing such payments has been written into bills before Congress. The passage of such a bill into law would have a major impact on the growth of private practice in counseling both in itself and because it would legitimize third-party payments by other major insurers such as Blue Cross. The speed with which the situation is changing is indicated by the fact that since the first edition of this book in 1986, Congress has authorized the payment of counselors by CHAMPUS, the agency that pays civilian practitioners for medical services performed for members of the military services and their dependents. But payments are made only to counselors who are licensed or certified.

LICENSURE AND CERTIFICATION

Implementation of third-party payment plans adds pressure to bring about strict licensure laws. In general, a license specifies the activities that a person in a given occupation can perform. Certification, which is similar, defines the standards that a person must meet in order to use a job title. Frequently, a license to practice is granted by a government agency while certification is controlled by an association of practitioners.

The term *counselor* is now defined in 41 states, although you can still see signs that read "Madame Zodiac—Palm Reading and Marriage Counseling." The first state licensure law was passed in Virginia in 1976. Since then, such laws have been passed in 40 other states, too. The addresses of the licensing boards for these states are listed in Appendix C or see *Journal of Counseling & Development* November/December 1995, p. 196.) and periodic updates in future issues.

Although laws do vary, among the common key provisions, from the point of view of a person planning to become a counselor, is graduation from a master's program accredited by the Council for Accreditation of Counseling and Related Educational Programs. These programs require forty-eight semester hours (as opposed to the thirty-three to forty hours required in most programs), a practicum lasting sixty contact hours, and an internship lasting three hundred contact hours; another option for certification is to have two years of experience and course work in six of the eight following areas: human growth and development; social and cultural foundations; the helping relationship; group dynamics, processing, and counseling; lifestyle and career development; appraisal of individuals; research and evaluation; and professional orientation. Under either option, candidates for certification must pass an exam, have three thousand hours of supervised counseling experience, and provide professional assessments from two colleagues or supervisors. Many other bodies offer certification of different kinds, and many counselors hold more than one certificate. The different boards are listed with the various counseling occupations and in Appendix C.

Licensure has many ramifications, not all of which are predictable at this time. For example, the standards may come to be applied to programs for school counselors as well as for those who wish to work in private practice or community agencies. Questions concerning reciprocity of state-recognized certificates and teaching requirements for counselors in educational settings are also frequently debated. Opposition to the laws is not unknown. It comes from local psychological associations in some cases; in at least one case, a rehabilitation services company opposed the legislation. A shortage of counselors would also undermine licensure. In a discussion of the employment trends for school psychologists, Thomas Fagan writes:

> Too large a discrepancy in supply and demand (e.g., 10–20 percent) would pose an unfortunate dilemma among the agencies and persons controlling training, credentialing, and practice. Unmet demand would trigger altered credential requirements for school-based employees. To maintain practical existence in the long-run, professional organizations could be forced to relax the progress for increased standards made in recent decades.

Some states have title laws, which control the definition and use of *counselor,* and other states have practice laws, which regulate the practice of a counseling specialty.

To summarize, the current trend is toward increasing licensure requirements, but the future is, as ever, uncertain.

COUNSELING, PSYCHIATRY, AND PSYCHOLOGY

Within guidance and counseling, there is a continuity between simply providing information and enabling a client to use the information, which might require techniques resembling psychotherapy. The principles of guidance and psychology are indeed closely related and, according to Nancy Scott, former Association for Counselor Education and Supervision president, confusion of the two continues. Where a particular counselor fits along the line depends on the nature of the problems that clients bring to him or her. Clients seeking to change careers, for example, rarely need to change the way they live. Clients who regularly overeat or abuse alcohol, however, must be helped to change their behavior, just as a psychiatrist's patients often must behave differently to be considered cured. What then is the difference between counseling and psychiatry or psychology?

The border between counseling and therapy is less like a wall than a seashore. Counseling does indeed make use of techniques developed by therapists; it just does not follow them as far. Counselors, for example, would usually see a client fewer times than a therapist would see a patient.

One difference is hidden in the previous sentence. Counselors have *clients;* psychiatrists and psychologists have *patients.* The people seen by a counselor are not regarded as mentally ill either by themselves or the counselor. Another distinction is that counselors deal with normal transitions and adjustments. A counselor who suspects someone is ill or severely affected by his or her condition will refer that person to an appropriate psychiatrist or psychologist.

More clear than the difference in practice is the difference in preparation. A psychiatrist must be a doctor of medicine. A psychologist or counseling psychologist must usually have a Ph.D. A counselor usually has a master's degree.

The waters are stirred up a little more by the term *psychoanalysis.* Strictly speaking, it refers to the method of treatment for the mentally ill developed by Sigmund Freud. Patients undergoing psychoanalysis make an intensive study of their own past, especially of events in their childhood that they no longer remember consciously. Counselors do not practice psychoanalysis. Loosely speaking, some counseling work may be referred to as *psychotherapy,* a term that includes psychoanalysis and other methods of treatment. But this term too is best restricted to situations where someone is being treated for mental or emotional disorder.

THE COUNSELOR'S ROLE

Like the relationship between counseling and psychology, the relationship between counseling and guidance in the school is subject to constant dispute; the American School Counselor Association's role statements are being rewritten even as this book is being published. Indeed, each specialty seems to have its own controversy over the counselor's role. Rehabilitation counselors are torn between counseling and coordinating services of other providers such as medical practitioners and welfare agencies. Employment counselors must constantly struggle to avoid becoming no more than test administrators. In the elementary schools, to give a final example, some see the counselor's chief duty as consulting with teachers rather than counseling children. None of these controversies is likely to be resolved anytime soon. Indeed, those that pit counselors against administrators will probably never be resolved. The most that someone entering the profession can hope to do is be aware of them.

CHAPTER 18

COUNSELING'S FUTURE

Good counselors lack no clients.

—Shakespeare

The social and technological developments that have changed so many occupations in recent years—increasing the demand for some, almost eliminating others, and changing the nature of the work in almost all—will also affect the future of counseling, although to what degree is largely a matter of speculation. At least two changes are certain: counselors will make greater use of computer technology and counselors will do more work with adults.

COMPUTERIZED COUNSELING

The impact of computers on counseling will probably be extensive. Their use in career education is already widespread, with many high school students being able to use computers to retrieve individualized information about colleges, training programs, and occupations with programs such as Career Focus. Already, more than half of all college planning/placement offices use computers for career guidance and counseling. Computers also shorten the time needed to assess aptitudes because tests taken at computer terminals can be scored almost instantly. The General Aptitude Test used by the Employment Service, the Armed Services Vocational Aptitude tests, and many others can now be taken at a computer terminal. Interactive programs such as MORTON and PLATO DCS are even available for psychodiagnosis. Their practicality may be limited because only clients comfortable with computer keyboards can use them at present, but people comfortable with computers, such as students, prefer them to pencil and paper.

Naturally, counselors can also use computers to ease their recordkeeping, data analysis, and word-processing burdens. One survey found that 75 percent of counselor educators now use computers for word processing.

Computers cannot replace the counselor, of course, any more than the once ballyhooed teaching machine was able to replace live instructors. In the words of the College Entrance Examination Board's Commission on Precollege Guidance and Counseling, "Computers . . . should be viewed as extensions of rather than substitutes for counselors, giving counselors more time for the activities that are central to their role." Counselors can use the machines to make more information available both to their clients and to themselves, but the essential work of the counselor—clarifying, instructing, and motivating—still remains. Paradoxically, computers might even increase the need for personal counseling because a computer printout of test results has greater credibility, and clients must be cautioned concerning their use. J. P. Sampson, for example, warns that computers make giving tests too easy, tempting untrained administrators to give and misinterpret them.

MORE WORK WITH ADULTS

The social changes taking place are likely to have a much deeper impact than the use of computers. Several trends are important. The number of older people is growing rapidly, and the average life span is lengthening. Conrad Glass and Katherine Brant note that these trends "are creating conditions that require the expansion of counseling services to a segment of the population often overlooked—the adult who is 65 years old and older." Gerontological counseling is now a specialty in its own right. A certification standard was approved in 1990. The middle-aged population is also growing as the baby-boom generation works its way through the life cycle. One result of that trend will be a much larger number of people switching careers in mid-life, either through choice or necessity; counseling can assist many of these people in clarifying their goals and learning what their options are. Changes in marital relationships and other concerns might also stimulate demand for counseling in this segment of the population. The result of these various trends is that the number and proportion of counselors working with adults will almost certainly increase. One sign of these changes has already been seen at the American Counseling Association. Its Association for Adult Development and Aging did not exist four years ago; it now has two thousand members.

Counselors working for agencies or in private practices that are obviously aimed at adults will not be the only ones affected by this trend. For example, many college and community college counselors will increasingly meet adults. These counselors will have to adapt themselves to the different needs of adult students, who are likely to be more anxious to complete their education speedily—especially if it is required for a new career—while also having greater family responsibilities and economic pressures than the traditional college-age population.

COUNSELORS IN NEW SETTINGS: PRIVATE SECTOR, PRIVATE PRACTICE

Many changes are foreseen in counseling: more gerontological counseling, more career counseling for adults, more mental health counseling. Indeed, Hollis and Wantz argue that the unmodified term *counselor* is becoming dated; now the reference is to specific kinds of counselors, such as those described in this book. As these changes occur, employment will shift away from the schools. Counselors already work in a great variety of settings: mental health agencies, rehabilitation agencies, correctional facilities, public employment agencies, health care facilities, employment assistance and human resource development programs in business and industry, and private practice. The variety of settings may not increase, but, in the opinion of many people in the field, the number of counselors employed outside the schools will, perhaps dramatically. In particular, most authorities expect to see more counselors employed by businesses and community agencies and many more entering private practice.

Although the extent of this growth is problematic, some developments along these lines have already taken place. For example, the enrollment of people in counselor education programs designed to prepare people for positions other than school counselor is now four times the enrollment in school counselor programs—which have, in fact, been declining for the past ten years. Surveys of graduates of counselor education programs also indicate that a substantial percentage are not working in schools. In one survey of more than a thousand graduates, over twice as many were employed outside the schools as in them. Graduates of a gerontological program were employed in state agencies, area agencies on aging, senior residence centers, mental health centers, and long-term care facilities.

Evidence also points toward more employment in business and more self-employment. Between 1950 and 1987, the number of employee assistance programs grew from about fifty to ten thousand. In 1990, about 50 percent of all large or medium size firms offered some sort of employee assistance program. Only a small percentage of mental health counselors work for employee assistance programs or in business settings, but these programs often refer employees to treatment programs where counselors work. Department stores even employ counselors to work with customers who have problems handling credit. Articles on career counseling for adults also indicate the change, for besides school-based programs, they are likely to list services sponsored by community agencies and private practices as sources of help. Perhaps the clearest sign of change is that the mental health division of the ACA—which did not even exist a few years ago—now has about twelve thousand members. Many of these counselors—perhaps 25 percent or more—are in private practice, as shown by a survey conducted by William Weikel, Richard Daniel, and Janet Anderson and by the ACA's annual survey of members.

CHAPTER 19

ADVICE FROM THE EXPERTS

In conducting the research for this book, I had the chance to speak to a large number of counselors in a variety of settings. At the end of each conversation, I asked them for advice, suggestions, or other comments they would like to make to someone who was considering a career in counseling. The following are their replies, listed alphabetically. Several years later, when I asked them if their remarks were still valid, most said that their statements should be even more forceful now.

> A growing field in vocational assessment and counseling is the rehabilitation area. Take a good look at it.
> —Olie Ahlquist, Past President, National Employment Counselors Association

> I've often found that people looking for a job do not know what that job entails. I'd recommend that you talk to a rehabilitation counselor—or a counselor in any other field that you are considering entering—and watch one at work, if possible.
> —Les Blankenship, Vocational Rehabilitation Program Specialist, Rehabilitation Services Administration, U.S. Department of Education

> Counseling and student affairs offer many career possibilities other than in the elementary and secondary school—

learn about them and try to explore them all. College students should seek out work experiences in student affairs.

—William A. Bryan, Past President, American College Personnel Association

Student affairs workers who like their jobs say they enjoy the environment of an institution of higher education, enjoy working with people, and enjoy the variety of contacts with students and faculty members.

—Jon Dalton, Assistant Vice-President for Student Affairs, Northern Illinois University

With regard to sex education and counseling, first seek an education in counseling, psychology, or social work; and then, after accumulating years of experience, you can try to specialize in human sexuality.

—Tom Gertz, Past President, American Association of Sex Educators, Counselors, and Therapists

If you are considering counseling as a career, ask yourself first how important freedom of choice for the individual is to you; if it's not of major importance, reconsider your career choice.

—Ken Hoyt, Kansas State University

Counseling will be on the cutting edge of assisting students to cope with the stress of the modern age so that they can fulfill their academic potential. With excellent training in all the new counseling skills, you will have many options— but you'll have to be skilled at working with families and the special concerns of today's young people: substance abuse, unemployment, teenage pregnancy, suicide, and all the others.

—Dorothy Jenkins, Past President, American School Counselor Association

Student affairs in community colleges is very competitive and has no clear career ladder, but it is full of challenges and rewards.

—John Keyser, President, Clackamas Community
College

The end result of rehabilitation in the private sector is to return the client to gainful employment. This requires that the counselor must develop close relations with employers; and to do that means you must understand business so that you can match their clients with individual employers. A counselor must also understand the legal system, because rehabilitation services are often delivered as a legal benefit within the insurance system.

—Richard LaFon, Past Executive Director, National
Association of Rehabilitation Professionals in the
Private Sector

In a field like financial aid—or student personnel generally—you must be ready for change, which is both the drawback and the satisfaction of the job.

—Dennis Martin, Director of Financial Aid, Washington
University

After looking at this book, quickly go out and find some working counselors who can give you first-hand experience about what the job is like. Get some part-time experience—even as a volunteer—in a variety of counseling settings.

—Carl McDaniels, Virginia Polytechnic Institute and
State University

Growth in social support occupations—such as rehabilitation and other counseling fields—will be very strong if our society continues to develop along the lines of one person's having several careers in a lifetime. The need for experts who can identify how a person's skills and aptitudes will fit new occupations could be substantial.

—Frederick E. Menz, The University of Wisconsin-Stout

Explore; start early—meet people through professional organizations, talk to them, and gain work experience.

—Fred Otte, Georgia State University

If you are thinking about becoming a pastoral counselor, first ask if you wish to serve people in the ministry, then ask if you wish to serve the ministry as a counselor.

—Duane Parker, Executive Director, Association for
Clinical Pastoral Education

A career decision begins with self-assessment. Learn about the occupation but learn also about your own needs and values. Volunteer experiences and talking to professional counselors about their work should help you learn if you'll find potential satisfaction in the work.

—Bill K. Richardson, North Texas State University

Every year, the responsibilities of school counselors grow, in keeping with their general mandate of promoting academic success for all students; we now deal with suicide prevention, child abuse, study skills, substance abuse, test-taking techniques, stress, anxiety, and drop-out and truancy prevention. This combination should make the demand for well-trained school counselors rise in the coming years. At the same time, the number of people being trained for educational settings is declining.

—Dr. Dorothy Thomas, Past President, American School
Counselor Association

School counselors in the future will probably have larger caseloads, making it more important than ever that you develop your skills as a consultant so that you can work with parents, teachers, and other school professionals in order to serve the students.

—Jean A. Thompson, Past President, American
Counseling Association and American School
Counselor Association

If you like to work with people, the satisfaction of counseling is great. The lengthening education and continuing education requirements should be considered, however; they will make it more difficult to become a counselor but might also increase the salaries and prestige of the profession in the long run.

—Edwin A. Whitfield, Director of School Guidance,
State of Ohio

You should seek to be highly competent and especially well trained in a variety of counseling techniques because of the changes now taking place in the delivery of, and payment for, mental health services.

—Richard R. Wilmarth, Chairperson, National Academy
of Certified Clinical Mental Health Counselors

The need for assessing an individual's skills and matching employers with employees will continue to be met in some way by our society, although the agencies that now utilize employment counselors may change.

—Gaynelle Wilson, Past President, National
Employment Counselors Association

A background in rehabilitation counseling can provide a springboard to the broader industry involved in containing the costs of health care—but you'll have to prod your graduate school into preparing you for the private sector.

—Jim Wilson, Past President, National Association of
Rehabilitation Professionals in the Private Sector

If you are considering becoming a rehabilitation counselor, try to enter an undergraduate rehabilitation feeder program—it can save a semester or more at the graduate level.

—George Wright, The University of Wisconsin, Madison

CHAPTER 20

CODA: COUNSELING, A HEALING PROFESSION

> Give a hungry man a fish and he can eat for a day; teach a
> hungry man to fish and he can eat all his life.

—Proverb

The glamour of heart surgery does not shine around counseling. "Counselors care," this book proclaims at its opening. And a cold world responds, "Who cares?" Ours is not an age of sensibility. We are a practical people concerned less with caring than with curing, less with helping than with healing. The challenge of counseling now and tomorrow will be to develop its potential to heal.

Richard Bolles, the author of *What Color Is Your Parachute?*, issued this challenge to the profession in a speech at the American Personnel and Guidance Association (now the ACA) convention in the early 1980s. He suggested that counseling could be content with service or could move on to empower people. "It is one thing," he said, "to throw a drowning person a rope. It is another to see a person in crisis and seize that as the moment to show them how to take control of the crisis, to teach them how to get out of the crisis for the rest of their lives."

He went on to refer to his well-known book, asking rhetorically why it is so successful. The book, after all, deals with what would seem to be the most pedestrian of counseling activities—finding a job—and it has no lack of competitors. Bolles pointed out that in reality *Parachute* is a book of healing; it only masquerades as a job-hunting manual. It heals the reader's self-esteem; it repairs the blow to their sense of worth when an employer says, "I don't need you; I don't want you!"

Like the rest of us, counselors are inundated by information and technological change. But more machines and more knowledge will not make counseling much more effective. "The future of counseling," Bolles concluded, "does not depend on mastering information or technology but in mastering ourselves as healers."

NATIONAL ASSOCIATIONS AND CERTIFICATION AUTHORITIES

Associations can provide three types of useful information for people interested in careers. First, they almost always publish a directory that will give you the names of nearby practitioners that you can talk with about the job. Second, their newsletters, journals, and other publications often contain want ads, articles about salaries and employment or other developments, and case studies based on actual situations that can give you insight into the nature of the work. Third, they sometimes publish pamphlets about occupations. The certification authorities publish registers of certified practitioners and booklets explaining the certification requirements. The accrediting authorities for educational programs are listed in the chapter on education.

A few of the associations listed here have such similar names that they may appear to be the same organization. Some of the apparent duplication is because of the character of a parent body; for example, the American Rehabilitation Counseling Association is specifically concerned with rehabilitation within the American Counseling Association, while the National Rehabilitation Counseling Association represents counselors within the National Rehabilitation Association.

American Counseling Association
  5999 Stevenson Avenue
  Alexandria, VA 22304
  (703) 823-9800

With more than fifty-four thousand members, this is the largest association of counselors in the country. It publishes the *Journal of Counseling and Development, Guidepost,* and many monographs and pamphlets. The Association has fifteen divisions and organizational affiliates that, in the words of its membership pamphlet, "span counseling and human development work at all educational levels from kindergarten through higher education, in community agencies, correctional agencies, rehabilitation programs, government, business/industry, and research facilities." The association does not provide financial aid or counseling services to individuals. The following are among its divisions and their publications.

- American College Counseling Association
- Association for Counselor Education and Supervision— *Counselor Education and Supervision; ACES Spectrum*
- National Career Development Association—*The Career Development Quarterly; NCDA Newsletter*
- Association for Humanistic Education and Development— *The Journal of Humanistic Education and Development; Infochange*
- American School Counselor Association—*The School Counselor; Elementary School Guidance and Counseling; The ASCA Counselor*
- American Rehabilitation Counseling Association—*Rehabilitation Counseling Bulletin; The ARCA News*
- Association for Assessment in Counseling and Development —*Measurement and Evaluation in Counseling and Development; AAC Newsnotes*

- National Employment Counselors Association—*Journal of Employment Counseling; NECA Newsletter*
- Association for Multicultural Counseling and Development —*Journal of Multicultural Counseling and Development; AMCD Newsletter*
- Association for Spiritual, Ethical, and Religious Values in Counseling—*Counseling and Values; ASERVIC Interaction*
- Association for Specialists in Group Work—*Journal for Specialists in Group Work; Together*
- American Mental Health Counselors Association—*Journal of Mental Health Counseling, AMHCA News*
- International Association of Addiction and Offender Counseling (IAAOC)—*Journal of Addictions & Offender Counseling; IAAOC Newsletter*
- Military Educators and Counselors Association—*MECA Newsletter*
- Association for Adult Development and Aging—*AADA Newsletter*

American Association for Marriage and Family Therapy
1133 15th Street, N.W., Suite 300
Washington, DC 20005
(202) 452-0109

The 16,500 members are drawn from several disciplines, including medicine and counseling. It publishes a bimonthly newspaper, a quarterly journal, and a biennial membership register.

American Association of Pastoral Counselors
9508A Lee Highway
Fairfax, VA 22031
(703) 385-6967

An association of more than three thousand ministers, priests, rabbis, and other religiously oriented counselors and professionals. It publishes a newsletter that lists job and training opportunities and *The Journal of Pastoral Care.*

American Association of Sex Educators, Counselors and Therapists
   435 North Michigan Avenue, Suite 1717
   Chicago, IL 60611
   (312) 644-0828

A multidisciplinary association of about three thousand physicians, psychologists, ministers, counselors, social workers, educators, marriage and family therapists, and others engaged in sex education, counseling, and therapy. It publishes a quarterly *Journal of Sex Education and Therapy,* a monthly newsletter, and an annual register of certified sex educators, sex counselors, and sex therapists.

American Psychological Association
   750 First Street, NE
   Washington, DC 20002
   (202) 336-5500

A society of scientists, teachers, and professionals organized to advance psychology (70,000 members). Membership is largely restricted to those who hold the doctorate. The concerns of counselors and members of the APA overlap at numerous points. The association has 45 divisions, at least four of which are directly related to counseling: Division 15, Educational Psychology; Division 16, School Psychology; Division 17, Counseling Psychology; Division 22, Rehabilitation Psychology. It publishes "Careers in Psychology," "Delivery of Services by Counseling Psychologists," and "Delivery of Services by School Psychologists" (single copies free) among many other items, including the following periodicals: *American Psychologist, Journal of Counseling Psychology, Journal of Educational Psychology, APA Monitor, The Educational Psychologist* (Division 15), *School Psychology Monograph* (Division 16), *The Counseling Psychologist* (Division 17), *Rehabilitation Psychology* (Division 22).

American Society for Training and Development
   1640 King Street
   Box 1443
   Alexandria, VA 22313
   (703) 683-8100

An association of 26,000 practitioners, managers, administrators, educators, and researchers in human resources development. Members design and implement employee and organization development programs in a broad range of business, education, government, and service organizations. It publishes a monthly magazine, *Training and Development Journal,* a monthly newspaper, *National Report on Human Resources,* directories of members and consultants, and numerous books. Members can join a professional practice area, one of which—career development—is for members who provide people and their organizations with guidance in the application of career development systems; they balance the needs of the employer and the employee so that the goals of both are met.

American Vocational Association
    1410 King Street
    Alexandria, VA 22314
    (703) 683-3111

This is a 46,000 member association of teachers and others interested in vocational education. Among its many divisions are ones devoted to employment and training and guidance. It publishes the monthly *Vocational Education Journal.*

College Placement Council, Inc.
    62 Highland Avenue
    Bethlehem, PA 18017
    (215) 868-1421

An association for career counseling and placement directors and representatives of employers of college graduates in business, industry, and government. The placement offices on college campuses often have copies of its publications if the library does not. It publishes *The Journal of Career Planning and Employment* (quarterly), *Spotlight* (a biweekly newsletter), a membership directory, as well as many other items.

Foundation for Rehabilitation Counseling Education
   1835 Rohlwing Road
   Rolling Meadows, IL 60008
   (847) 394-1785

This board certifies and provides information concerning the certification of rehabilitation counselors and insurance rehabilitation specialists.

Independent Educational Consultants Association
   4085 Chain Bridge Road, Suite 401
   Fairfax, VA 22030
   (703) 591-4850

An association of educational counselors in private practice. It publishes a membership directory.

National Academy of Certified Clinical Mental Health Counselors
   5999 Stevenson Avenue
   Alexandria, VA 22304
   (703) 823-9800

This board certifies clinical mental health counselors. It has 12,000 members and publishes the quarterly *Journal of Mental Health Counseling.* Certification may be required for third-party payment.

National Association of Alcoholism and Drug Abuse Counselors
   3717 Columbia Pike
   Suite 300
   Arlington, VA 22204
   (703) 920-4644

The 11,000 members of this association work in hospitals, treatment centers, private practice, councils and agencies on alcoholism and drug abuse, and employee assistance programs. It publishes *The Counselor,* a biennial magazine.

National Association of Rehabilitation Professionals in the Private Sector
   313 Washington Street, Suite 302
   Newton, MA 02158
   (617) 558-5333

An association of rehabilitation counselors and the firms they work for in the private sector. It publishes a code of ethics and a bimonthly newsletter, *NARPPS News.*

National Association of School Psychologists, Inc.
   4340 East West Highway, Suite 402
   Bethesda, MD 20814-4411
   (301) 657-0270

An association for school psychologists (18,980 members). It publishes *School Psychology Review* (quarterly) and a newsletter.

National Association of Student Activity Advisers
   1904 Association Drive
   Reston, VA 22090
   (703) 860-0200

A 53,000 member association of directors of student activities, deans, and others affiliated with student activity programs in middle schools and high schools. It publishes *Leadership for Student Activities* (monthly) and other material.

National Association of Student Financial Aid Administrators
   1920 L Street, NW, Suite 200
   Washington, DC 20036
   (202) 785-0453

An association of institutions and financial aid administrators with 3,500 members. It publishes a newsletter and the *Journal of Student Financial Aid.*

National Association of Student Personnel Administrators, Inc.
   1875 Connecticut Avenue, NW, Suite 418
   Washington, DC 20009
   (202) 265-7500

An association of 6,500 student affairs officers in postsecondary institutions and interested graduate students. Publications include the *NASPA Forum* (its newsletter) and an annual salary survey.

National Association of Substance Abuse Trainers and Educators
    1521 Hillary Street
    New Orleans, LA 70118
    (504) 861-4756

A relatively small association of academic, state, and federal trainers (about 100 members) who voluntarily exchange information on substance abuse/chemical dependency training in higher education with respect to courses, student populations, degree programs, nondegree programs, and graduate studies. The major activity of the association is to sustain a clearinghouse of training and educational opportunities.

National Board for Certified Counselors, Inc.
    3 Suite D Terrace Way
    Greensboro, NC 27403
    (910) 547-0607

This board certifies counselors who have voluntarily sought certification and maintains a register. It offers both a generic certification and a specialized certification for career counselors. This certification does not constitute a license to practice in states that have passed counselor licensure legislation.

National Rehabilitation Counseling Association
    8807 Sudley Road, Suite 102
    Manassas, VA 22110
    (703) 361-2077

Part of the National Rehabilitation Association, it has 4,400 members. It publishes the quarterly *Journal of Applied Rehabilitation Counseling.*

BOOKS ABOUT COLLEGE, GRADUATE SCHOOL, CAREERS, AND COUNSELING

The following two selective lists contain two kinds of books. The first has general works for job hunters and career seekers, including a couple of books on selecting a college and scholarships. The second has books about counseling. Several are used as a text in an introductory course; they provide insight into the methods used in counseling and the concerns counselors deal with.

GENERAL BOOKS ON COLLEGE AND CAREERS

American Universities and Colleges. Washington, D.C.: American Council on Education. annual.

Bloch, Deborah Perlmutter. *How to Make the Right Career Moves.* Lincolnwood, Ill.: VGM Career Horizons, 1990. Step-by-step details on how to advance in your career.

_____ . *How to Have a Winning Job Interview.* Lincolnwood, Ill.: VGM Career Horizons, 1991. Advice on how to win an interview and get a job.

_____ . *How to Write a Winning Résumé.* Lincolnwood, Ill.: VGM Career Horizons, 1989. Filled with tips and examples.

Bolles, Richard N. *What Color Is Your Parachute? A Practical Manual for Job-Hunters and Career-Changers.* Berkeley, Calif.: Ten Speed

Press, 1993 (but new editions frequent). Quite possibly the most frequently recommended guide to finding a career (not just a job).

Chronicle Guide to Graduate and Professional Study. Moravia, N.Y.: Chronicle Guidance Publications, Inc. biennial.

The College Handbook Index of Majors. Princeton, N.J.: College Board Publications. annual.

A Guide to Graduate Study. Washington, D.C.: American Council on Education. frequent editions.

Kennedy, Joyce Lain and Darryl Laramore. *Joyce Lain Kennedy's Career Book.* 2d ed. Lincolnwood, Ill.: VGM Career Horizons, 1992. Covers deciding what you want to do, moving on from your present job, and everything in between.

Lott, Catherine S. and Oscar C. Lott. *How to Land a Better Job.* Lincolnwood, Ill.: VGM Career Horizons, 1994. Covers everything from finding leads to negotiating salaries.

Lovejoy's College Guide. Red Bank, N.J.: Lovejoy's College Guide, Inc. frequent editions.

Michelozzi, Betty Neville. *Coming Alive from Nine to Five.* Palo Alto, Calif.: Mayfield Publishing Co., 1991. Career planning, with exercises for self-assessment.

Need a Lift? Indianapolis: The American Legion. An annual hundred-page plus listing of current information on careers, loans, and scholarships.

Peterson's Guides: Graduate Study. 4 vols. Princeton, N.J.: Peterson's Guides. annual.

Rubinfeld, William A. *Planning Your College Education.* Lincolnwood, Ill.: VGM Career Horizons, 1991. Discusses choosing and gaining admission to college.

U.S. Department of Labor. *Occupational Outlook Handbook.* Washington, D.C.: Government Printing Office. biennial. Considerable information on 225 occupations, counseling and psychology among them. It has updated information on employment, salaries, and occupational outlook.

BOOKS ABOUT COUNSELING

Brown, Jeannette A. and Robert H. Pate, Jr., eds. *Being a Counselor.* Monterey, Calif.: Brooks Cole, 1983.

Burks, Mary Paxton. *Requirements for Certification: Teachers, Counselors, Librarians, Administrators, for Elementary Schools, Secondary Schools, Junior Colleges.* 51st ed. Chicago: University of Chicago Press, 1988.

Carnevale, J. *Counseling Gems: Thoughts for the Practitioner.* Muncie, Ind.: Accelerated Development, 1989.

Doyle, Robert E. *The Essential Skills and Strategies in the Helping Process.* Pacific Grove. Calif.: Brooks Cole, 1992.

Gysbers, Norman and associates. *Designing Careers.* San Francisco: Jossey-Bass, 1984. This is a third decennial review of career counseling put together by the National Association for Career Counseling and Development, formerly the National Vocational Guidance Association. The contributors, a virtual who's who of the field, include Norman Gysbers, C. Gilbert Wrenn, Donald E. Super, Harold Goldstein, Edwin L. Herr, Johnie H. Miles, Howard E. Figler, Carl McDaniels, and many others.

Gysbers, Norman C. and P. Henderson. *Developing and Managing Your School Guidance Program.* Alexandria, Va.: American Association for Counseling and Development, 1988.

Herr, Edwin L. *Counseling in a Dynamic Society: Opportunities and Challenges.* Alexandria, Va.: American Association for Counseling and Development, 1989.

Liberty, Leona H. *Counselor: National Certification and State Licensing Preparation.* New York: Simon & Schuster, 1990.

May, Rollo. *The Art of Counseling.* New York: Gardner Press, 1989.

Mortensen, Donald and Alan Schmuller. *Guidance in Today's School.* 3d ed. New York: John Wiley and Sons, 1976.

Pietrofesa, John J., et al. *Counseling: An Introduction.* 2d ed. Boston: Houghton Mifflin, 1984.

Shertzer, Bruce and Shelley C. Stone. *Fundamentals of Counseling.* 3d
    ed. Boston: Houghton Mifflin, 1981.

Super, Donald E. and Charles M. Super. *Opportunities in Psychology
    Careers.* Lincolnwood, Ill.: VGM Career Horizons, 1988. A complete
    guide to the work of psychologists, including school psychologists,
    and ways to start out in the field.

Thompson, Charles L. and Linda B. Rudolph. *Counseling Children.* 2d
    ed. Pacific Grove, Calif.: Brooks Cole, 1988.

STATE ACCREDITING AND LICENSING AUTHORITIES

State agencies govern the licensing and certification of most types of counselors. This appendix contains addresses of state authorities that regulate professional school counselors, agencies charged with mental health and family counseling, and those agencies or designated organizations that license or accredit the growing specialty of substance abuse counselors. The list of school counseling authorities was drawn from information supplied by the American Counseling Association, and was compiled by ACA's Office of Government Relations in June 1996. Later updates can be had from ACA, 5999 Stevenson Ave, Alexandria VA 22304, (703) 823-9800. The information on other accrediting bodies (mental health counseling, marriage and family therapy) was drawn from sources such as the National Board for Certified Counselors, Greensboro, North Carolina and the American Association for Marriage and Family Therapy. Information on addiction counseling was also received from substance abuse agencies and the Certification Reciprocity Consortium/Alcoholism and Other Drug Abuse, Inc. Other types of counselors should contact professional associations or state governments in their locales to find out about state accrediting and licensing rules.

Alabama

Alabama Board of Examiners in Counseling
Walter Cox, Executive Officer
P.O. Box 550397
Birmingham, AL 35255

Department of Education
Gordon Persons Office Building
50 North Ripley Street
Montgomery, AL 36130–3901

Alaska

Department of Education
801 West 10th Street, Suite 200
Juneau, AK 99801–1894

Alaska Alcohol and Drug Abuse
Counselor Certification Review Board
3605 Arctic Boulevard #695
Anchorage, AK 99503

Arizona

Arizona Board of Behavioral Health Examiners
David Oake, Executive Director
c/o Counseling Credentialing Committee
1400 West Washington Street, Suite 350
Phoenix, AZ 85007

Department of Education
1535 West Jefferson
Phoenix, AZ 85007

Arkansas

Arkansas Board of Examiners in Counseling
Ann K. Thomas, Executive Director
Southern Arkansas University
Box 1396
Magnolia, AR 71753–5000

Department of Education
   Arch Ford Education Building
   Four Capitol Mall
   Little Rock, AR 72201–1071

Arkansas Substance Abuse Certification Board
   P.O. Box 962
   North Little Rock, AR 72115

California

Board of Behavioral Science Examiners
   Kathleen Callanan, Executive Officer
   400 R Street, Suite 3150
   Sacramento, CA 95814–6240

Department of Education
   721 Capitol Mall
   P.O. Box 944272
   Sacramento, CA 94244–2720

California Association of Alcohol and Drug Abuse Counselors
   1713 J Street, Suite 207
   Sacramento, CA 95814

Colorado

State Board of Licensed Professional Counselor Examiners
   Joan Seggerman, Administrative Assistant
   1560 Broadway, Suite 1340
   Denver, CO 80202

Department of Education
   201 East Colfax Avenue
   Denver, CO 80203–1799

Connecticut

Department of Education
   165 Capitol Avenue
   Hartford, CT 06106

Connecticut Alcohol and Drug Abuse Counselor Certification Board
   416 New London Turnpike
   Glastonbury, CT 06033

Delaware

Board of Professional Counselors of Mental Health
   Gayle Franzolino, Administrative Assistant
   Cannon Building
   P.O. Box 1401, Suite 203
   Dover, DE 19903

Department of Public Instruction
   Townsend Building
   P.O. Box 1402
   Dover, DE 19903

Delaware Alcohol and Drug Abuse Counselor Certification Board, Inc.
   P.O. Box 9937
   Newark, DE 19714–9937

District of Columbia

D.C. Board of Professional Counselors
   Dr. C. Yvonne Crawford, Administrator
   605 G Street NW, Room LL–202
   Washington, DC 20001

Board of Education
   415 12th Street, NW, Suite 1205
   Washington, DC 20004

Washington Metropolitan Area Counselor Certification Board
   2001 O Street, NW
   Washington, DC 20036
   (Alcohol and Drug Abuse Counselors)

Florida

Agency for Health Care Administration
   Board of Mental Health Counselors
   Lola Pouncey, Administrator
   1940 North Monroe Street
   Tallahassee, FL 32399–0753

Department of Education
   The Capitol PL–08
   Tallahassee, FL 32399

Certification Board for Addiction Professionals of Florida
    835B East Park Avenue
    Tallahassee, FL 32301

Georgia

Composite Board of Professional Counselors, Social Workers &
        Marriage & Family Therapists
    Examining Boards Division
    Lori Gold, J.D., Director
    166 Pryor Street, SW
    Atlanta, GA 30303

Department of Education
    2060 East Twin Towers
    205 Butler Street, SE
    Atlanta, GA 30334–5010

Hawaii

Department of Education
    P.O. Box 2360
    Honolulu, HI 96804

Idaho

Idaho State Counselor Licensing Board
    Bureau of Occupational Licenses
    Janice Wiedrick, Board Secretary
    Owyhee Plaza
    1109 Main Street, Suite 220
    Boise, ID 83702–5642

Department of Education
    850 West State Street, Room 200
    P.O. Box 83720
    Boise, ID 83720–0027

Illinois

Illinois Department of Professional Regulations
  Mary Wright, Board Liaison
  320 West Washington Street
  Springfield, IL 62786

State Board of Education
  100 North First Street
  Springfield, IL 62777–0001

Illinois Addiction Counselor Certification Board
  104 North 4th Street
  Springfield, IL 62701

Indiana

Department of Education
  229 State House
  Indianapolis, IN 46204

Indiana Counselor Association on Alcohol and Drug Abuse, Inc.
  1800 North Meridian Street, Suite 507
  Indianapolis, IN 46202

Iowa

Iowa Department of Public Health, Bureau of Professional Licensed
    Behavioral Science Examiners
  Carol Barnhill, Board Administrator
  Lucas Building, 4th Floor
  Des Moines, IA 50319

Department of Education
  Grimes Building
  Des Moines, IA 50319–0146

Iowa Board of Substance Abuse Certification
  P.O. Box 7284
  Grand Avenue Station
  Des Moines, IA 50309

Kansas

Behavioral Sciences Regulatory Board
    Cheryl H. Kinderknecht
    712 South Kansas Avenue
    Topeka, KS 66603–3817

Board of Education
    120 SE 10th Avenue
    Topeka, KS 66612

Kansas Alcohol and Drug Abuse Counselors Association
    P.O. Box 1732
    Topeka, KS 66601

Kentucky

(Law passed 1996; until board is established, contact:)
    Kentucky Counseling Assocation
    622 Timothy Drive
    Frankfort, KY 40601

Department of Education
    Capital Plaza Tower
    500 Mero Street
    Frankfort, KY 40601

Kentucky Chemical Dependency Counselors' Professional Certification
        Board
    P.O. Box 21891
    Lexington, KY 45022–1891

Louisiana

Licensed Professional Counselors
    Board of Examiners
    Lin Falcon, Administrative Assistant
    4664 Jamestown Avenue, Suite 125
    Baton Rouge, LA 70808–3218

Department of Education
    P.O. Box 94064
    Baton Rouge, LA 70804–9064

Certification Examining Board of LASCAT, Inc.
  P.O. Box 80235
  Baton Rouge, LA 70898-0235
  (Alcohol and Drug Abuse Counselors)

Maine

Maine Board of Counseling Professionals Licensure
  Mary Breton, Board Clerk
  State House Station, #35
  Augusta, ME 04333

Department of Education
  23 State House Station
  Augusta, ME 04333

Maryland

State of Maryland
  Department of Mental Health/Hygiene Professional Counselors
  Aileen Taylor, Administrator
  Metro Executive Center, 3rd Floor
  4201 Patterson Avenue
  Baltimore, MD 21215–2299

Department of Education
  200 West Baltimore Street
  Baltimore, MD 21201

Maryland Addictions Counselor Certification Board
  P.O. Box 3341
  Frederick, MD 21701

Massachusetts

Board of Allied Mental Health & Human Services Professions
  Emily Mitchell, Chairperson
  100 Cambridge Street, 15th Floor
  Boston, MA 02202

Department of Education
  350 Main Street
  Malden, MA 02148–5023

The Massachusetts Committee for Voluntary Certification of Alcoholism
Counselors, Inc.
560 Lincoln Street
P.O. Box 7070
Worcester, MA 01605

Michigan

Michigan Board of Counseling
Doris Foley, Licensing Administrator
P.O. Box 30018
Lansing, MI 48909

State Board of Education
P.O. Box 30008
Lansing, MI 48909

Michigan Institute for Human Resources Development
B–304 Ellsworth Hall
Western Michigan University
Kalamazoo, MI 49008
(Alcohol and Drug Abuse Counselors)

Minnesota

Department of Children, Families, and Learning
Personnel Licensing Section
616 Capitol Square Building
550 Cedar
St. Paul, MN 55101

Institute for Chemical Dependency Professionals of Minnesota, Inc.
596 South Osceola Avenue
St. Paul, MN 55102

Mississippi

Mississippi State Board of Examiners for Licensed Professional
Counselors
Glenda Jenkins, Executive Secretary
1101 Robert E. Lee Building
239 North Lamar Street
Jackson, MS 39201

Department of Education
    P.O. Box 771
    Jackson, MS 39205

Mississippi Association of Alcohol and Drug Abuse Counselors
    P.O. Box 3507
    Meridian, MS 39303

Missouri

Division of Professional Registration
    Committee for Professional Counselors
    Becky Stirling, Executive Director
    3605 Missouri Boulevard
    P.O. Box 162
    Jefferson City, MO 65109

Department of Elementary & Secondary Education
    205 Jefferson Street
    P.O. Box 480
    Jefferson City, MO 65102–0480

Missouri Substance Abuse Counselor Certification Board
    P.O. Box 1673
    Columbia, MO 65205

Montana

Board of Social Work Examiners & Professional Counselors
    Mary C. Hainlin, Administrative Assistant
    Arcade Building
    111 North Jackson
    Helena, MT 59620

Office of Public Instruction
    106 State Capitol
    P.O. Box 202501
    Helena, MT 59620–2501

Nebraska

Bureau of Examining Boards
    Kris Chiles, Associate Director
    301 Centennial Mall South
    P.O. Box 95007
    Lincoln, NE 68509–5007

Department of Education
    301 Centennial Mall South
    P.O. Box 94987
    Lincoln, NE 68509–4987

Nevada

Department of Education
    700 East Fifth Street
    Carson City, NV 89710

New Hampshire

Board of Psychology
    Peggy Lynch
    105 Pleasant Street
    Box 457
    Concord, NH 03301

Department of Education
    101 Pleasant Street
    Concord, NH 03301

New Hampshire Office of Alcohol and Substance Abuse Prevention
    6 Hazen Drive
    Concord, NH 03301

New Jersey

New Jersey Division of Consumer Affairs
    Board of Professional Counselors
    Leslie Aronson
    P.O. Box 45007
    Newark, NJ 07101

Department of Education
  225 East State Street
  CN 500
  Trenton, NJ 08625–0500

New Jersey Alcoholism Counselor Certification Board
  90 Monmouth Street, Suite 202
  Red Bank, NJ 07701

New Jersey Substance Abuse Counselor Certification Board
  (same address as above listing)

New Mexico

New Mexico Counseling & Therapy Practice Board
  Regulation & Licensings Department
  Juanita M. Uhl, Administrator
  1599 St. Francis Drive
  Santa Fe, NM 87504

Department of Education
  Education Building
  300 Don Gaspar Street
  Santa Fe, NM 87501–2786

New Mexico Alcohol and Drug Abuse Counselor Association
  Certification Board
  7711 Zuni Road, SE
  Albuquerque, NM 87108

New York

Department of Education
  Education Building
  Washington Avenue
  Albany, NY 12234

North Carolina

North Carolina Board of Licensed Professional Counselors
  Lucinda Chew
  Box 21005
  Raleigh, NC 27619–1005

Department of Public Instruction
    301 North Wilmington Street
    Raleigh, NC 27601–2825

North Dakota

North Dakota Board of Counselor Examiners
    P.O. Box 2735
    Bismarck, ND 58502

Department of Public Instruction
    State Capitol
    11th Floor
    600 East Boulevard Avenue
    Bismarck, ND 58505–0440

Ohio

Counselor & Social Worker Board
    Beth Farnsworth, Executive Secretary
    77 South High Street, 16th Floor
    Columbus, OH 43266

Department of Education
    65 South Front Street
    Columbus, OH 43266–0308

Ohio Chemical Dependency Counselors Credentialing Board, Inc.
    274 Marconi Boulevard, Suite 420
    Columbus, OH 43215

Oklahoma

Licensed Professional Counselors Committee
    Mike Blazi, Administrator
    1000 NE 10th Street
    Oklahoma City, OK 73117–1299

Department of Education
    2500 North Lincoln Boulevard
    Oklahoma City, OK 73105–4599

Oklahoma Association on Alcohol and Other Drug Abuse
Counselor Certification Board
2248 North Moore Avenue
Moore, OK 73160

Oregon

Oregon Board of Licensed Professional Counselors & Therapists
Carol Fleming, Board Administrator
3218 Pringle Road SE #160
Salem, OR 97302–6312

Department of Education
Public Service Building
255 Capitol Street, NE
Salem, OR 97310–0203

Pennsylvania

Department of Education
333 Market Street
Harrisburg, PA 17126–0333

Pennsylvania Certified Addiction Counselors Board
4751 Lindle Road, Suite 113
Host Inn
Harrisburg, PA 17111–9986

Rhode Island

Department of Health
Cannon Building
Division of Professional Regulation
Peter Petrone, Administrative Officer
Mental Health Counselor
3 Capitol Hill, Room 104
Providence, RI 02908–5097

Department of Elementary & Secondary Education
22 Hayes Street
Providence, RI 02908

South Carolina

South Carolina Department of Labor Licensing Regulations
    Division Professional & Occupational Licensing
    Marjorie Montgomery, Administrator
    3600 Forest Drive, Suite 101
    P.O. Box 11329
    Columbia, SC 29211–1329

Department of Education
    1429 Senate Street, Room 1006
    Columbia, SC 29201

South Dakota

South Dakota Board of Counselor Examiners
    Jamie L. Post, Executive Secretary
    115 East Sioux
    P.O. Box 1115
    Pierre, SD 57501

Department of Education & Cultural Affairs
    700 Governors Drive
    Pierre, SD 57501–2291

South Dakota Chemical Dependency Counselors Certification Board
    P.O. Box 102
    Yankton, SD 57078

Tennessee

Tennessee State Board of Professional Counselors & Marital & Family
        Therapists
    Virginia Jenkins, Board Administrator
    283 Plus Park Boulevard
    Nashville, TN 37247–1010

Department of Education
    Gateway Plaza
    710 James Robertson Parkway, 6th Floor
    Nashville, TN 37243–0375

Texas

Texas State Board of Examiners for Professional Counselors
Kathy Craft, Executive Secretary
1100 West 49th Street
Austin, TX 78756–3183

Education Agency
1701 North Congress Avenue
Austin, TX 78701–1494

Texas Certification Board for Alcohol and Drug Abuse Counselors
5510 IH North
Austin, TX 78751

Utah

Brigham Young University
Dr. Ronald Bingham
328 McKay Building
P.O. Box 25093
Provo, UT 86402

Education Office
250 East 500 South
Salt Lake City, UT 84111

Utah Association of Alcohol and Drug Abuse Counselors
P.O. Box 26332
Salt Lake City, UT 84126

Vermont

LCMHC Advisory Board
Dianne LaFaille, Staff Assistant
109 State Street
Montpelier, VT 05609–1106

Department of Education
120 State Street
Montpelier, VT 05620–2501

Vermont Alcoholism and Drug Abuse Counselor Association
    P.O. Box 562
    Newport, VT 05855

Virginia

Virginia Board of Professional Counselors
    Department of Health Professionals
    Evelyn Brown, Executive Director
    6606 West Broad Street, 4th Floor
    Richmond, VA 23230

Department of Education
    James Monroe Building
    101 North 14th Street
    P.O. Box 2120
    Richmond, VA 23216–2120

Washington

Health Professions Section 2
    Department of Health
    Tracy Robecker
    P.O. Box 47869
    Olympia, WA 98504–7869

Department of Public Instruction
    Old Capitol Building
    P.O. Box 47200
    Olympia, WA 98504–7200

West Virginia

West Virginia Board of Examiners in Counseling
    West Virginia Graduate College
    Charles Maine, Administrator
    100 Angus East Payton Drive
    South Charleston, WV 25303–1600

Department of Education & the Arts
  State Capitol Complex
  Building 1 Room R–151
  1900 Kanawha Boulevard East
  Charleston, WV 25305

West Virginia Alcoholism and Drug Abuse Counselor Certification Board
  P.O. Box 1257
  Morgantown, WV 26507

Wisconsin

Wisconsin Department of Regulation Licensing
  Betsy Wood
  P.O. Box 8935
  Madison, WI 53708

Department of Public Instruction
  P.O. Box 7841
  Madison, WI 53707–7841

Wisconsin Alcoholism and Drug Abuse Counselor Certification Board,
    Inc.
  416 East Main Street
  Waukesha, WI 53186

Wyoming

Mental Health Professions Licensure Board
  Veronica Skoranski, Administrative Officer
  First Bank Plaza
  2020 Carey Avenue, Suite 201
  Cheyenne, WY 82002

Department of Education
  Hathaway Building
  2300 Capitol Avenue, 2nd Floor
  Cheyenne, WY 82002–0050

A complete list of titles in our extensive *Opportunities* series

OPPORTUNITIES IN

Accounting
Acting
Advertising
Aerospace
Agriculture
Airline
Animal & Pet Care
Architecture
Automotive Service
Banking
Beauty Culture
Biological Science
Biotechnology
Broadcasting
Building Construction Trades
Business Communications
Business Management
Cable Television
CAD/CAM
Carpentry
Chemistry
Child Care
Chiropractic
Civil Engineering
Cleaning Service
Commercial Art & Graphic
    Design
Computer Maintenance
Computer Science
Computer Systems
Counseling & Development
Crafts
Culinary
Customer Service
Data & Word Processing
Dental Care
Desktop Publishing
Direct Marketing
Drafting
Electrical Trades
Electronics
Energy
Engineering
Engineering Technology
Environmental
Eye Care
Farming and Agriculture
Fashion
Fast Food
Federal Government
Film
Financial
Fire Protection Services

Fitness
Food Service
Foreign Language
Forestry
Franchising
Funeral Services
Gerontology & Aging Services
Health & Medical
Heating, Ventilation, Air
    Conditioning, and
    Refrigeration
High Tech
Home Economics
Homecare Services
Horticulture
Hospital Administration
Hotel & Motel
Human Resources
    Management
Information Systems
Installation & Repair
Insurance
Interior Design & Decorating
International Business
Journalism
Laser Technology
Law
Law Enforcement &
    Criminal Justice
Library & Information
    Science
Machine Trades
Marine & Maritime
Marketing
Masonry
Medical Imaging
Medical Sales
Medical Technology
Mental Health
Metalworking
Military
Modeling
Music
Nonprofit Organizations
Nursing
Nutrition
Occupational Therapy
Office Occupations
Optometry
Paralegal
Paramedical
Part-Time & Summer Jobs
Performing Arts
Petroleum
Pharmacy

Photography
Physical Therapy
Physician
Physician Assistant
Plastics
Plumbing & Pipe Fitting
Postal Service
Printing
Property Management
Psychology
Public Health
Public Relations
Publishing
Purchasing
Real Estate
Recreation & Leisure
Religious Service
Research & Development
Restaurant
Retailing
Robotics
Sales
Science Technician
Secretarial
Social Science
Social Work
Special Education
Speech-Language Pathology
Sports & Athletics
Sports Medicine
State & Local Government
Teaching
Teaching English to Speakers
    of Other Languages
Technical Writing &
    Communications
Telecommunications
Telemarketing
Television & Video
Theatrical Design &
    Production
Tool & Die
Training & Development
Transportation
Travel
Trucking
Veterinary Medicine
Visual Arts
Vocational & Technical
Warehousing
Waste Management
Welding
Writing
Your Own Service Business

VGM Career Horizons
a division of *NTC/Contemporary Publishing Company*
4255 West Touhy Avenue
Lincolnwood, Illinois 60646–1975